exploring HEAVENLY PLACES

Power in the Heavenly Places

VOLUME 4

PAUL L. COX
BARBARA KAIN PARKER

EXPLORING HEAVENLY PLACES
Power in the Heavenly Places
Volume 4

Paul L. Cox and Barbara Kain Parker

Aslan's Place Publications
9315 Sagebrush
Apple Valley, CA 92308
760-810-0990

www.aslansplace.com

Unless otherwise noted, all scripture quotations are from the New King James Version of the Bible. Copyright © 1979, 1980, 1982 by Thomas Nelson, Inc., publishers. Used by permission.

Greek definitions are derived from Strong's Greek Concordance.
Hebrew definitions are derived from Strong's Hebrew Concordance.
Copyright 2015, by Paul L. Cox and Barbara Kain Parker
All rights reserved.
Cover design and layout by Brodie Schmidtke
ISBN # 978-1-5136-1986-6
Printed in the United States of America

TABLE OF CONTENTS

INTRODUCTION

As I (Barbara) considered how to write the Introduction and put together the chapters of *Exploring Heavenly Places, Volume 4*, the Lord led me to Psalm 19, which is sub-titled, *The Perfect Revelation of the LORD* in the NKJV. There could be no better introduction to the content of this book, as we explore manifestations of God's power that originate in heavenly places and manifest on the earth.

> *The heavens declare the glory of God;*
> *And the firmament shows His handiwork.*
> *Day unto day utters speech,*
> *And night unto night reveals knowledge.*
> *There is no speech nor language*
> *Where their voice is not heard.*
> *Their line has gone out through all the earth,*
> *And their words to the end of the world.*
> *In them He has set a tabernacle for the sun,*
> *Which is like a bridegroom coming out of his chamber,*
> *And rejoices like a strong man to run its race.*
> *Its rising is from one end of heaven,*
> *And its circuit to the other end;*
> *And there is nothing hidden from its heat.*
> *The law of the LORD is perfect, converting the soul;*
> *The testimony of the LORD is sure, making wise the simple;*
> *The statutes of the LORD are right, rejoicing the heart;*
> *The commandment of the LORD is pure, enlightening the eyes;*
> *The fear of the LORD is clean, enduring forever;*
> *The judgments of the LORD are true and righteous altogether.*
> *More to be desired are they than gold,*
> *Yea, than much fine gold;*
> *Sweeter also than honey and the honeycomb.*
> *Moreover by them Your servant is warned,*
> *And in keeping them there is great reward.*
> *Who can understand his errors?*
> *Cleanse me from secret faults.*
> *Keep back Your servant also from presumptuous sins;*
> *Let them not have dominion over me.*
> *Then I shall be blameless,*

And I shall be innocent of great transgression.
Let the words of my mouth and the meditation of my heart
Be acceptable in Your sight,
O LORD, my strength and my Redeemer.

The heavens certainly do declare God's glory! His handiwork is evident everywhere we look throughout the earth, and scriptures are full of golden nuggets of truth that may not have been previously recognized because our everyday focus is usually on what we see right in front of us. But, as Moses' tabernacle was a prophetic look at the heavenly version, so are the manifestations of God's power a hint of the glorious eternity that awaits those who are His.

1

CHAPTER ONE

Discerning God's Power

It was the much publicized, end-of-the-world day, December 21, 2012. The world was filled with expectation for something dramatic to occur. It was a long day of unknown possibilities, but nothing happened, and life went on as usual for most people. That was not the case with me (Paul), for on that day I began discerning someone new. Exploring all the possibilities I could think of, I found no confirmation of any. I spoke to many individuals about what I was feeling and a lot of them said that they were sensing the same thing, but none of us could determine what it was. Two weeks passed and it was now 2013, when a 'suddenly' occurred and I realized that I was discerning the Person of the Holy Spirit. After twenty-two years of learning to identify many spiritual beings through discernment, I was now being taught to recognize the Holy Spirit as a person.

About a month later, I was praying for a woman who was having difficulty with an attack from a fallen spiritual being. Even though she had previously experienced significant deliverance, she was unable to gain victory over this entity. As we talked, I asked her to point to where she could see the being. She indicated that it was in the corner of the room, so I walked over to it and discerned a fallen son of God. She relayed to me that the being was very arrogant and would not respond, even to the blood of Christ. I was mystified, and troubled that I could think of no solution for her predicament, so I asked the Lord what to do and had a sense to ask Jesus to come as the Son of Man and wage war against this fallen son. Immediately, the woman saw Jesus riding in on a white horse. He rode over to the entity and, with a swipe of a huge sword; the fallen son of God was destroyed. As Jesus was moving, I realized that I could discern Him in a new way as the Son of Man. Now, both the Holy Spirit as a person and Jesus as the Son of Man could be identified through discernment.

Three months passed, and I had a sense that we were to have a gathering on Pentecost. Three days before, an email invitation went out for people to join us either at Aslan's Place or via the web. A friend responded, saying that he felt the Lord wanted to take us from Acts 2 to Acts 4, but what might that mean?

On Friday night, around 35 of us came together, with over 150 more online. We began praying, and suddenly I felt a surge of power come on me. I could discern tongues of fire on each of us, and I also experienced another new discernment. It felt like someone had grabbed the back of my neck and was squeezing it like one would squeeze a lemon. Many others also felt the presence. As we enquired of the Lord, He revealed that we were discerning the Father as the Power. I remembered a verse that had intrigued me many years ago, Matthew 26:64, in which Jesus was responding to the high priest at His trial:

> *Jesus said to him, "It is as you said. Nevertheless, I say to you, hereafter you will see the Son of Man sitting at the right hand of the Power, and coming on the clouds of heaven."*

Now, here we were on the day of Pentecost, over two thousand years later, and the Father gave us discernment about His Power that illuminated our understanding of Acts 1:8 in a new way:

> *But you shall receive power when the Holy Spirit has come upon you; and you shall be witnesses to Me in Jerusalem, and in all Judea and Samaria, and to the end of the earth.*

I had always understood the verse to mean that when the Holy Spirit comes, you will receive the power of the Holy Spirit. Is it possible that what we are really being taught is that when the Holy Spirit comes we will gain revelation of the Father as the Power?

In moving from Acts 2 to Acts 4, the Father took us from the reception of the power of God to a demonstration of Himself as the Power:

> *Now the multitude of those who believed were of one heart and one soul; neither did anyone say that any of the things he possessed was his own, but they had all things in common. And with great power the apostles gave witness to the resurrection of the Lord Jesus. And great grace was upon them all. Nor was there anyone among them who lacked; for all who were possessors of lands or houses sold them, and brought the proceeds of the things that were sold, and laid them at the apostles' feet; and they distributed to each as anyone had need.*[1]

Many in the church of Jesus Christ are longing for a return of an Acts-like demonstration of the power of the Father, the Son, and the Holy Spirit. What we have not understood is that God's power is coming, but it will manifest in ways that we haven't anticipated. In fact, as we look back over the years, we see that we have already been surprised again and again as the Lord has manifested His power in some of the most unexpected ways.

2

CHAPTER TWO

The Manifest Power of God

When I (Paul) think of power, I immediately consider massive explosions, gigantic earthquakes, overpowering tsunamis, destructive volcanoes, and colossal hurricanes. All of these are certainly evidences of power, but in reality the word, 'power', simply means the 'ability to do or act; capability of doing or accomplishing something'.[1]

Pondering God's power, I tend to recall first the displays of His glorious power in miraculous demonstrations in public meetings where people have been literally knocked off their feet by His amazing presence. This has become fairly common, and truly is a work of His power; but just as real is His power to do or to act in ways we could never anticipate or coordinate. As we consider God's power, much of our discussion entails the tangible power that we discern, and the victorious display of His authority against His enemies, but there are other indications of His power that bring constant surprises to our daily lives. Carl's story, which happened in the nineties, is a great example of God's power manifesting in one person's life.

Carl came to our house for a youth Bible study in which I was leading a generational prayer session. He stayed after everyone left, and we started a discussion. He said he was a generational Mormon but had gone into Buddhism, and he had been astral projecting. I began talking to him about the Lord, but the discussion quickly turned into a theological argument. Then I suddenly had an idea, and asked him if I could try something. He agreed, and I said, "Anger, come forth." He started manifesting, his eyes rolling back in his head; so I told him to come to the front. Looking at me, he asked, "What was that?" I replied, "That is what is controlling you." He asked what to do, and I said, "Give your life to Christ." As he did, I actually felt the Holy Spirit rushing into him. That night he went home and started speaking in tongues, and we later led him in several more prayer sessions.

This was in the early years of my growth in deliverance ministry, and the Lord was teaching us to deal with many levels of deliverance. One day my daughter called and said that Carl was at work, but something had overcome him. I called, but could not talk to him because the entity said it now controlled him. Later, meeting at a restaurant, the entity continued to speak through his mouth, saying that he knew who I was as well as claiming to have created the world and brought all the people up to the high desert. I did not know what to do, but suggested that we go to my house. He came, and the Lord gave me a verse, which I proclaimed and he was set free. Unfortunately, I do not remember which verse.

Carl later married, but the marriage did not last and he moved back to the Salt Lake area. I could not understand what had happened to him, but the weekend before September 11, 2001, I was just outside of Salt Lake City, Utah when a man came up to me and said, "Carl says, 'Hi.'" I asked if Carl was the same man I had known in the high desert, and he confirmed that he was. I was astonished, and very happy to hear that the man had been disciplining Carl for quite awhile. It seems he never lost his faith, and he now operates in a high level of the prophetic, lives in Idaho, and is involved in the new move of God. What a wonderful display of the Power of God to change a life!

It was February 8, 2008, and I was praying for a person at Aslan's Place. Looking through the window in front of me, I saw a young eaglet sitting on the bottom branch of the pine tree just outside. Stunned, I asked the prayer partner to look and she verified that, indeed, an eaglet was sitting on the branch. How was this possible since many cats roam the area? I could not remember ever seeing an eagle around our home, let alone one that was perched outside my window! The eaglet looked into my eyes, raised it wings and flew off. I walked outside to examine the tree, and there was such anointing on it! Then I remembered the date—February 8, 2008, or 2-8-08—two eights. Eight refers to a new beginning, so this date indicated a double new beginning. What kind of power could arrange this?

In early 2015, we had just returned to LAX from Hawaii where the Lord had come in great power during the Sunday night service. As people walked through a new gate of time, many fell under His power, and the Lord proclaimed to us that he was moving us out of man's time into His Kairos time. Now, back in Los Angeles, as we approached the baggage claim area to retrieve our luggage I noticed that one of our suitcases was already going around on the carousal. My first impression was that it had appeared far too soon because we had just exited the plane, but I retrieved the first item while Donna waited at the door of the terminal. Then I looked up, and there was our second piece of luggage; and then the third appeared. I noticed that no one else had anything yet, and nothing else was arriving on the carousal. Moving our things over to meet Donna at the door, and looking back—still no other luggage had arrived. We went to the curbside and waited a few minutes for our friend to meet us with the car. After loading our bags and ourselves into the car, we started to drive away and I looked again, but the carousal remained empty. What had just happened? How had our luggage arrived? I left the airport amazed at God's power.

The number seven refers to divine perfection or spiritual completion. On January 12, 2014 (7 + 7 = 14 = two sevens), I had my seventieth (perfect spiritual order) birthday. On that same day our seventh grandchild, who was born on January 12, 2007, celebrated his seventh birthday. I had also just finished writing my seventh book, and the next day seven of us went in a van to Disneyland. Is such a display of sevens not another evidence of God's power? It certainly wasn't co-incidence!

There is no end to God's power, but it seems that our understanding of it is ever increasing. During a recent Exploring Heavenly Places meeting, a friend received a faith-filled word that brings an expectation of seeing His Power come in greater measure than ever before:

> Power of the age to come; power that you have not seen or tasted
> yet, for I will take a stand against the wicked and the nations. Power
> that will teach them to fear and to humble themselves again, for wick-

edness has arisen from the nations. Far too long, I have tested and seen the hearts and spirits of man. Now, I am about to take a stand. There will be hope again for those who fear My name, hope for the generations to come. I will blow away the chaff of the weak, the branching that you have not even seen and can't tell because they are [aligned] with the covenant of death. All you can see is the fruit. My people try to chop off the root, and I am the God who can chop off the root. This is the day I will make a stand in the midst of the congregation. Kingdoms will fall; My light over all [and] you will become the beacon of light; the city on a hill, the city that shall not disappear. Your fruit shall stay. He will heal the hearts that are disappointed.

It is my prayer that as we continue our journey into heavenly places we will all:

> ...*know Him and the power of His resurrection, and the fellowship of His sufferings, being conformed to His death.*[2]

3

CHAPTER THREE

A Taste of Honey

We all have our own idiosyncrasies in regard to food. Some like it hot, some like it cold; some like meat and potatoes, some like salads; some love chocolate and can't comprehend why others don't. When I (Barbara) say I don't like honey, people look at me like I'm crazy. Who in their right mind doesn't like honey? Me! So I was very surprised when an angel showed up in a dream and gave me a jar of honey to eat. Hesitant at first, I tasted it and was amazed that I liked it—in fact, it was delicious. I was especially glad to have learned that I do enjoy the heavenly version when, shortly thereafter at a Come Up Higher conference in Fresno, honey manifested in the Spirit and we were instructed to eat it.

Sometime around 1987, Paul had his first significant spiritual encounter as he read Proverbs 12:13-14:

> *Eat honey my son, for it is good; honey from the comb is sweet to taste. Know also that wisdom is sweet to your soul; if you find it, there is a future hope for you, and your hope will not be cut off.*

At the time he didn't know what an anointing was, let alone what it felt like, so he likened the experience to having bells and whistles going off in his head. Years later he received a prophetic word for 2010, which included the same verses.

Within a few weeks honey was referenced again in another word:

> There is no turning back…we are rediscovering something. There is new revelation…you will confirm it in scripture. It is the pure honey of the Word.

> *How sweet are Your words to my taste, sweeter than honey to my mouth!* [1]

In prior years there had been other references to honey:

> (April 2005) Receive from the tree of life; receive the honeydew— the dew from heaven that is like honey.

> (March 2006) Discernment is being dispensed…receive what is being dispensed to you. The honey. The dew. Receive the manna.

> *And the house of Israel called its name Manna…and the taste of it was like wafers made with honey.* [2]

> (October 2006) You cannot go back…unity brings a cup of gold and He's going to pour out gold and honey of revelation over us…the angel is pouring gold and honey over us.

During a time of exploration and revelation in November 2008, a lady received in the Spirit a large vat of honey and invited all to taste and see. A sense of unity became increasingly evident as everyone began embracing one another and offering personal insights regarding the manifestation of honey. Paul asked, "What does this have to do with honey?" The replies included:

> It's strength for the battle.

> When you talk about protection, I still see a honeycomb but it's dripping.

> Honey means provision.

Honey was always healing for me.

Paul continued, "It never deteriorates, nor does it get contaminated. Is the honeycomb inside the mighty ones? We've seen the yellow light inside the tree; and honeycombs are in the trees." The reference to the mighty ones is further clarified by Paul's description of his initial encounter with them.

> I was in North Carolina a few years ago when the Lord first revealed the mighty ones. I perceived something in front of me and we got the words, 'mighty ones'. People saw them like cedar trees with hollow centers. They appeared to change shape into men with gold helmets with red and purple feathers, and honey dripping down over them. We also noticed that our faces were hot.

> > *Lift up a banner on the high mountain…I have also called My mighty ones for My anger…The LORD of hosts musters the army for battle…from the end of Heaven—the LORD and His weapons of indignation, to destroy the whole land…all hands will be limp, every man's heart will melt, and they will be afraid…their faces will be like flames.[3]*

References to honey during episodes of revelation are consistent with the accounts of both Ezekiel and John:

> *So I ate, and it was in my mouth like honey in sweetness, and the little book… was as sweet as honey in my mouth.[4]*

During a ministry session in July 2010, after a very unpleasant ungodly depth was discerned and the word was received:

> Now we are being taken out…flying, going to a place of revelation. Now the dark place is gone. Lord, we praise and exalt Your name. It's a heavenly place. I am being taken through a honeycomb. My people have judged the time by the darkness. They have decided their position according to the darkness. Their perception was too small…their understanding led them into darkness…into false perceptions.

The word aligns with Psalm 19:9-11:

> *The fear of the LORD is clean, enduring forever; The judgments of the LORD*

are true and righteous altogether. More to be desired are they than gold… Sweeter also than honey and the honeycomb.

The person who had been receiving ministry obtained significant healing, illustrating again the properties of honey:

Pleasant words are like a honeycomb, sweetness to the soul and health to the bones.[5]

In April 2011, honey began manifesting on hands. Paul wrote in an email:

I have been having spiritual honey show up in my hands recently. It is very sticky. It happened the first day of the conference and again yesterday during deliverance. I do not fully understand why. Is it tied to a new level of deliverance???

This happened again at Sagebrush Ranch in June, with most of us examining our shiny, sticky hands in awe; and about a week later at Collingwood Canada, Mimi Lowe[6] observed as, "an angelic being is pouring stuff on each one of us. Like honey..."

In May 2011, the Lord took several of us into new realms of deliverance in regard to ungodly generational trading. At one point, Paul discerned a whirlwind swarming with flies that had to do with Beelzebub[7] coming off of the generational line and he felt nauseous. He asked the Lord to apply honey, and immediately he not only felt better but also discerned that the whirlwind had stopped, and thousands upon thousands of flies were coming off and rushing upward. Could this be spiritual evidence of the strengthening effects of honey in the physical realm, such as the brightening of Jonathon's countenance after he dipped into a honeycomb and ate the honey?[8]

We've seen that the eating of honey is a pleasurable, and even life-sustaining experience, yet the wise father of Proverbs uses it as an example as he encourages his son to balance the pursuit of pleasure with the pursuit of wisdom, and to seek pleasure in moderation.[9] Honey may also symbolize sexual pleasure, in both positive and negative connotations.[10]

Your lips, O my spouse, Drip as the honeycomb; Honey and milk are under your tongue…I have eaten my honeycomb with my honey.

...for the lips of an immoral woman drip honey.

Honey continued to manifest, and in 2013 Crystal Kain Ross[11] had a couple of visions that illuminated our understanding further. In the first, she saw Paul Cox and 49 other intercessors in a heavenly court where they received stone tablets.

> [The stone tablets] were similar in size, 24 inches tall, 18 inches wide, and 12 inches thick. I was instructed to look closer, and immediately, I could see inside them. They were soft gray, and very porous, and the internal structure was completely honeycombed. The outside was similar to a hard rock that had gone through many intense fires; thereby producing the honeycomb structures inside...they did not have writing on the outside, but I was told the information would be placed inside...[A heavy golden liquid was poured into each tablet and they were sealed]...Then we were immediately transported above the Western Wailing Wall in Jerusalem. The sun was setting. I was told it was the beginning of Passover in Jerusalem.

> Each person was told to touch the bottom of their honey-filled stone tablets, which then began glowing red (symbolizing Jesus' shed blood)...They were told to raise their hands in declaratory praise and statutory orations, which were accompanied by many angelic counterparts...It was a solemn, glorious, and very loud and moving explosion of sound. It felt as if many things were being displaced and removed, and at the same time, many things were being placed and rooted...the stones fell in an exact straight line, making a perfectly-spaced square...embedded in the concrete about 6 inches deep, as effortlessly as if falling into soft dirt. When the stone tablets hit the ground, the holy honey contents spilled forth. The honey behaved like a mighty breath was behind it, moving over the ground to the outer edges, like water flowing effortlessly, instead of as how honey normally behaves...the spoken words took on actual substance and shape and, landing on the honey, they immediately arced into purple mini-fires, which all joined to each other on the top of the honey, covering the ground and making the appearance of a solid square ring of burning holy honey.

> As the smoke from the honey rose up, it was very concentrated,

and was most aromatic and lovely. It smelled like earthly honey, but enhanced with many extra heavenly scents, and it felt as if the smoky vapors contained intrinsic, extremely concentrated elements of mercy and healing.

Then Jesus said, "Here then are the explanations of what you have seen. The honey which was poured into the stone tablets represents the latter gold rain I've promised in the form of wisdom, revelation, and encased in a covering of My deliverance and mercy."

Three days later, Crystal had another vision in which she observed 33 angels and 3 key intercessors. A large golden bowl, five feet wide and so heavy that it required several angels to carry it, was brought forward. The bowl was lined with brass, rimmed with silver, and contained a mixture of oil and honey. Crystal reported:

The aroma of the honey-oil mix smelled so good—healing good. It was heavenly honey and oil, not earthly, and reminded me of what I had seen before at the beginning of Passover when the 50 stone tablets had held the honey and oil mixture. I wondered if it were the same substance.

Three more days passed, and Paul was conducting a discernment session in which the conversation concerned our ongoing spiritual battle. Someone first had a word about flint, and then Paul recalled a prophetic word he had received (his words in parentheses):

On flinty rock...I am the rock, and razor perfect...I have propelled you upward to ever increasing height...(which is what I think the Lord is doing today)... because you have sought my wisdom more than man searches for gold or fame...therefore, I've decreed to you that I release oil and honey mix; and then you shall continue to search forth, and from out of my summits where you are found upon My flinty rock. It is a firm foundation, impenetrable, unmovable...(I think this is talking about all of us)...others have come to the mountain, but not sought My wisdom. However, you've not been after experience, but after Me and have sought wisdom, but not to pump yourself up with knowledge. (Flinty rock and height; now isn't that interesting in light of the Song of Moses?)

He made him ride in the heights of the earth, that he might eat the produce of the fields; He made him draw honey from the rock, and oil from the flinty rock.[12]

(Oil from the flinty rock—that was in the word that she gave me, talking about honey and oil from the flinty rock. Look at it. It's all there; honey, oil from the flinty rock, and heights. This is all tied together with the battle, with perseverance, with the Lord coming to our rescue. I get the word that the battle is the Lord's and not ours.)

The value of honey cannot be understated—there are 20 NKJV references to Canaan as a land flowing with milk and honey,[13] as well as multiple scriptures that designate honey as a precious gift or valuable commodity.[14]

In Isaiah's prophesies, both of the eventual coming of Immanuel and imminent destruction, his references to honey would seem to illustrate deprivation; but I prefer to view it as God's provision in the midst of tragedy. How much worse things would have been without it!

[She] shall call His name Immanuel. Curds and honey He shall eat...The LORD will bring the king of Assyria upon you...It shall be in that day that a man will keep alive a young cow and two sheep; so it shall be, from the abundance of milk they give, that he will eat curds; for curds and honey everyone will eat who is left in the land.[15]

Some might also view John the Baptist's diet of locusts and wild honey with a sense of deprivation. But how much better to realize that John, as the forerunner of Jesus, was simply living out prophetically the teaching of his Lord that had yet to be spoken:

Then Jesus said to His disciples, "If anyone desires to come after Me, let him deny himself, and take up his cross, and follow Me."[16]

Honey—such a common substance that most of us take for granted. Yet, it is clear that it represents much more of the power and glory of God, and it often manifests in His presence.

4

CHAPTER FOUR

God's Weather Report

The familiar words are uttered frequently in weather reports: thunder, lightning, wind, rain, clouds, tornados, whirlwinds, hail, rainbows, hurricanes, the eye of the storm, etc. The images we attach to each word or phrase allow us to immediately comprehend what's going on in the world, but how often do we pause to consider the spiritual ramifications of these same weather-related elements?

> *Then He also said to the multitudes, "Whenever you see a cloud rising out of the west, immediately you say, 'A shower is coming'; and so it is. And when you see the south wind blow, you say, 'There will be hot weather'; and there is. Hypocrites! You can discern the face of the sky and of the earth, but how is it you do not discern this time?"* [1]

Science often confirms and explains much of God's creation and, while the vast majority of it goes way over my head, I (Barbara) do remember learning in elementary school about the water cycle. Also known as the hydrologic cycle, it is water's circle of evaporation, condensation, precipitation, and flow back into the ocean. It's a complex scientific process, but the basics are fairly simple to understand; water evaporates off the earth, condenses into clouds, falls back to earth as mist, rain, hail, or snow; it drains into streams and rivers that flow back to the oceans; and the process continually repeats itself.

> *A generation goes, and a generation comes, but the earth remains forever. The sun rises, and the sun goes down and hastens to the place where it rises. The wind blows to the south and goes around to the north; around and around goes the wind, and on its circuits the wind returns. All streams run to the sea, but the sea is not full; to the place where the streams flow, there they flow again.*[2]

Add winds to the water cycle, and we're right back to those afore-mentioned weather reports that tell of coming storms, droughts from lack of rain, and high wind advisories. But from a spiritual perspective, perhaps, the Bible could be viewed as God's weather report, providing both historic and prophetic perspectives of weather-related issues:

> *Behold, God is great, and we do not know Him;*
> *Nor can the number of His years be discovered.*
> *For He draws up drops of water,*
> *Which distill as rain from the mist,*
> *Which the clouds drop down*
> *And pour abundantly on man.*
> *Indeed, can anyone understand the spreading of clouds,*
> *The thunder from His canopy?*
> *Look, He scatters His light upon it,*
> *And covers the depths of the sea.*
> *For by these He judges the peoples;*
> *He gives food in abundance.*
> *He covers His hands with lightning,*
> *And commands it to strike.*
> *His thunder declares it,*
> *The cattle also, concerning the rising storm.*[3]

> *Therefore thus says the LORD GOD: "I will cause a stormy wind to break forth in My fury; and there shall be a flooding rain in My anger, and great hailstones in fury to consume it.*[4]

> *For He commands and raises the stormy wind,*
> *Which lifts up the waves of the sea.*
> *They mount up to the heavens,*

They go down again to the depths;
Their soul melts because of trouble.
They reel to and fro, and stagger like a drunken man,
And are at their wits' end.
Then they cry out to the LORD in their trouble,
And He brings them out of their distresses.
He calms the storm,
So that its waves are still.[5]

Then He arose and rebuked the wind, and said to the sea, "Peace, be still!" And the wind ceased and there was a great calm…And they feared exceedingly, and said to one another, "Who can this be, that even the wind and the sea obey Him!"[6]

After these things I saw four angels standing at the four corners of the earth, holding the four winds of the earth, that the wind should not blow on the earth, on the sea, or on any tree.[7]

Scriptures are very clear, God is in control in both the heavens and on the earth, and His majesty and power is exhibited throughout His creation, including the weather. As the Lord has unwrapped some of His mysteries for us, He has also surprised us with the spiritual realities of some of those familiar words and phrases from our local weather reporter.

Not surprisingly, we've received many 'storm warnings' over the years, three of which are submitted here. On November 24, 2008, Larry Pearson[8] heard an angel's message:

Fresh revelations. There will be waterspouts of new revelatory understandings as we gather; new waterspouts will open. You will then become the word of revelation. You and the word will become one. You are My message. Well done, well done to run; well done; go run; well done; come run with me on all the mountains. I will glean every mountain and I will loose my mighty warriors and angels to be on all the mountains. They will occupy land and the kingdoms of this world are becoming the kingdoms of Jesus Christ. This is a kingdom thing…A great churning and a great turning, spiritual hurricanes are coming. Spiritual hurricanes are coming. A storm of glory, a storm of glory is at hand. Storms of confusion will confound that which is false, that which is wicked, that which has set itself up against Father's knowledge...The eyes of the Lord are moving to and fro, looking out among the earth, among the Americas. Is there anyone strong enough; is there anyone that has My eagle eye that I might show myself mighty through?

On May 10, 2010, at an advanced discernment session there had been a tongue spoken and I received the following interpretation and message:

The tongue is a lament. The time of lamenting is over. And as the earth shakes, as the heavens shake, as all that can be shaken is shaken, you My people will not be shaken. It's a new day. I heard the song, *Joy Comes in the Morning*. We are to enter into His rest and stay there. From His rest there will be no lamenting. We will be moving about in joy.

As the earth shakes, as the heavens shake, as nations fall, as catastrophes happen in the physical—economic storms, earthquakes, everything that is to come—we will not be shaken. We've already been shaken. We've been shaken to our foundation, and now we can stand when everything else is falling apart.

This is how I will call all people unto Me. I speak through My children. You are My children. You will speak My words and I will draw all people unto Me because all of the dross has been removed and you will be able to stand. You will be able to point the way to Me because I am the only answer.

People will seek answers from the government. They will not find them. They will seek answers from doctors. They will not find them. They will seek answers from places they sought before but they will not find them. I am the only answer. I am the Truth, the Way, I am the Light and I shine through you. I will draw all men to Myself through you, My children. So enter into the rest and partake of My joy, and a lot of the joy that will well up in you is because you will finally see results.

Dawn Bray[9] received an angelic message on July 10, 2013:

A storm is coming; do not fear

What you will see, you will also hear
I've given you a door
I've given you a key
But what is inside you're about to see
Water flows in; water flows out
What you heard was a shout
As Achsah said, it shall be and it will be a part of what you see
As lightening flashes across the sky
The fire you see comes from within my eye
There is a wall, but do not dig for the hole is already there and it is big
Do not trespass on this land for it is sinking sand
Use the key that I will give you and that is what will break you through

As we examine the scriptures alongside the prophetic words, two things are immediately and abundantly clear. First, The Lord may speak to us out of a storm, as He did to Israel; and second, unlike Israel, we must heed the admonitions throughout scripture to not be afraid.

Now all the people witnessed the thunderings, the lightning flashes, the sound of the trumpet, and the mountain smoking; and when the people saw it, they trembled and stood afar off. Then they said to Moses, "You speak with us, and we will hear; but let not God speak with us, lest we die." And Moses said to the people, "Do not fear; for God has come to test you, and that His fear may be before you, so that you may not sin." [10]

Fear not, for I am with you;
Be not dismayed, for I am your God.
I will strengthen you,
Yes, I will help you,
I will uphold you with My righteous right hand.[11]

5

CHAPTER FIVE

The Power of the Whirlwinds

My (Paul's) life has been filled with transitions. After leaving the Baptist world of hymns and choruses, I discovered a new realm of worship music that was greatly influenced by the Vineyard and Calvary Chapel. Instead of singing about God, I learned to sing to God. One song that was very popular in the early nineties has recently come back into my thoughts. In those earlier days, I had no idea that I would eventually experience a realm of His power beyond my understanding.

Kevin Prosch, the composer of *Show Your Power*, wrote:[1]

> He is the Lord, and He reigns on high (He is the Lord)
> Spoke into the darkness created the light (He is the Lord)
> Who is like unto Him never ending in days (He is the Lord)
> And He comes in power when we call on His name (He is the Lord)
>
> Show Your power, O Lord my God
> Show Your power, O Lord my God
>
> Your gospel, O Lord is the hope for our nation (You are the Lord)

It's the power of God for our salvation (You are the Lord)
We ask not for riches but look to the cross (You are the Lord)
And for our inheritance, give us the lost (You are the Lord)

Send Your power, O Lord my God
Send Your power, O Lord my God

We sang these words numerous times, begging the Lord to show His power; and time after time He answered our plea, but not as we expected. His response came in a series of demonstrations of ever-increasing power. We would experience a new level of His power, adjust ourselves to the wonderful manifestation of His Glory, and then He would surprise us with an even greater level. In the fall of 2013, we began to touch something much stronger than we had felt before, but it would not be until October 2014, that the reality of this power came into clear focus.

I had been invited to speak at a conference in 2013. On Sunday afternoon I had already realized that I had no direction for the evening service when the conference organizer came into my motel room to discuss what we would do. As we talked, we began feeling a whirlwind, so after he left I started researching scriptures about the whirlwind. That evening, we had barely started the service when the power of God became evident, leaving us so stunned that we simply invited people to come forward, and I just sat and watched what the Lord was doing as He took us into the heavens. This was a brand new experience to many people, a first taste of what it's like to explore the heavenly realms or dimensions. Some began to see and hear with their spiritual eyes and ears, and discernment manifested as others reported sensations in their five physical senses, such as smelling heavenly fragrances, tasting honey, and physically feeling the presence of angels.

Since then, whenever we taught on the whirlwinds of God we would often feel the whirlwind, but had not yet really understood its full reality.

In October 2014, the Lord suddenly exposed the 'golden pipes'[2], and we discerned that they were located in a complex system of spiritual realities that were surrounded by the whirlwind. As I discerned the pipes, I put my hand about 18 inches away in front of me. No matter what direction I would place my hand; I could feel the movement of air traveling from right to left in a counter-clockwise direction. At rest, the whirlwind would simply circle around, but every time I prayed deliverance for a person the whirlwind seemed to speed up and carry the evil away. I no longer felt the evil leaving as I had before, but instead discerned deliverance by putting my hand into the whirlwind. A new level of God's power had been revealed.

I love confirmation of what the Lord is doing, and on October 24, 2014, one year after our first encounter with the whirlwind, Chuck Pierce made a declaration that the Hebrew New Year of 5775 (the year of *Ayin Hei*) would be the year of the whirlwind. In his email on that date he showed many examples of actual whirlwinds around the world.

We have also observed that the whirlwind may often feel very cold. I first discerned this coldness when I felt the 'cloud of His Glory'. When Ezekiel saw the whirlwind coming out of the north he described his vision:

> *Then I looked, and behold, a whirlwind [supa] was coming out of the north, a great cloud with raging fire engulfing itself; and brightness was all around it and radiating out of its midst like the color of amber, out of the midst of the fire.*[3]

It would seem that the cloud and the whirlwind are closely related, which is why we often discerned the coldness. On October 22, 2014, I had a dream in which it was summer but the temperature was only one degree Fahrenheit. I believe this dream was speaking to me about the coldness of the cloud of His Glory.

There are two key Old Testament Hebrew words that are translated into the English word 'whirlwind':

1. *Sûpâ*, which means storm wind (Isaiah 5:28; Hosea 8:7). The basic meaning of this verb is reflected in ASV, RSV, whereas KJV has 'be consumed'. It is used of God's judgment (Psalm 73:19; Jeremiah 8:13; Amos 3:15), especially in the end of things (Isaiah 66:17; Zephaniah 1:2f.), and of the unending annual observation of Purim (Esther 9:28).[4]

2. *Sā'ar*, which means storm, whirlwind, tempest, windstorm. The word is used to describe a literal storm (Ps 107:25ff; 148:8), sometimes as a symbol of God's judgment (Isaiah 29:6). Its use as a theophany (Job 38:1; 40:6) renders more understandable Elijah's translation into heaven in a whirlwind (II Kgs 2:1). It is used as 'to storm', as in during Jonah's sea

flight (Jon 1:11ff.). Taking its meaning from a physical storm, *sā'ar* usually appears in contexts of upheaval and distress. Hosea (13:2-3) warns the Israelites of his day that because of their idolatry, God would send them away into exile as chaff driven by a 'tempest' (cf. Zechariah 2:8-14), Isaiah (54:11-14) prophesies that the God of all grace and compassion will yet restore his 'storm'-tossed and troubled people and establish them in righteousness in a land of unsurpassing beauty and safety.[5]

As we look at the scriptures that contain 'whirlwind', we observe the tremendous power of the whirlwind and its use by the Almighty in judging and annihilating evil.[6]

...from the chamber of the south comes the whirlwind [supa], and cold from the scattering winds of the north. By the breath of God ice is given, and the broad waters are frozen. Also with moisture He saturates the thick clouds; He scatters His bright clouds. And they swirl about, being turned by His guidance, that they may do whatever He commands them on the face of the whole earth. He causes it to come, whether for correction, or for His land, or for mercy.[7]

When your terror comes like a storm, and your destruction comes like a whirlwind [supa], When distress and anguish come upon you. "Then they will call on me, but I will not answer; they will seek me diligently, but they will not find me. Because they hated knowledge and did not choose the fear of the LORD, they would have none of my counsel and despised my every rebuke. Therefore they shall eat the fruit of their own way, and be filled to the full with their own fancies. For the turning away of the simple will slay them, and the complacency of fools will destroy them; but whoever listens to me will dwell safely, and will be secure, without fear of evil." [8]

When the whirlwind [supa] passes by, the wicked is no more, but the righteous has an everlasting foundation.[9]

The nations will rush like the rushing of many waters; but God will rebuke them and they will flee far away, and be chased like the chaff of the mountains before the wind, like a rolling thing before the whirlwind [supa].[10]

...scarcely shall they be planted, scarcely shall they be sown, scarcely shall their stock take root in the earth, when He will also blow on them, and they will wither, and the whirlwind [saar] will take them away like stubble.[11]

When you see this, your heart shall rejoice, and your bones shall flourish like grass; the hand of the LORD shall be known to His servants, and His indignation to His enemies. For behold, the LORD will come with fire and with His chariots, like a whirlwind [supa], to render His anger with fury, and His rebuke with flames of fire. For by fire and by His sword the LORD will judge all flesh; and the slain of the LORD shall be many.[12]

These scriptures reveal that the scope of God's power in the whirlwind is very evident, playing a dramatic role as He establishes righteousness and justice upon the earth.

6

CHAPTER SIX

Unfolding Revelation of Whirlwinds

Since completing my (Paul) BA in History and English from Pepperdine University, I have had a sense of history, realizing that not only do we study history, but we also live in events that certainly will become historical to those who follow us. With this in mind, I have endeavored to record all the dreams and words given to me by others. This has proven to be beneficial when new revelation comes and I realize that what the Lord is currently showing us has previously been prophesied. When the first revelation of the whirlwind came I searched through my documents and was astonished at what I found. I would like to share these words, the first of which was over ten years ago! Please also note that these words give us an indication of further revelation about the whirlwinds that might be coming.

March 14, 2005, Mimi Lowe:

> Whirlwind, whirlwind, whirlwind, whirlwind
> Revelation coming, revelation coming, revelation coming
> You're going to dip into the pool
> Let go, let go, let go, let go!

You've never been there before; you've never been there before!
There's another well, there's another well, there's another well
Unearth the well, unearth the well, and unearth the well
Jump in, jump in, jump in!
Bring your children in; bring your children in!

August 13, 2007, Robin Shannon[1] saw whirlwinds and oaks of righteousness.

Acceleration in due time
We're oaks of righteousness
Whirlwinds of acceleration picking us up, and we're skipping and
jumping over
We're running and not being weary
We're speeding up into God's time
Invite the whirlwinds
It's a wall of fire, spinning away the bad, the impurities
The glory comes in
He wants us to be hit with lightning
In order for this to happen the living water has to flow and to get rid
of the impurities
He must spin us

April 14, 2007, Jana Green:[2]

Zion waits. Come to the mountain of the Lord. Be taught by the
Lord. You have not known your authority…the wealth of the ages
awaits. Come and get it…the righteousness is before you. The
Lord is your rear guard…it is a new mindset, the Kingdom mindset.
Riches in Glory, heavenly currency; it is in the whirlwind.

June 4, 2008, Mimi Lowe:

Whirlwind. I am sending a whirlwind to remove the debris in your
life. For you have been commissioned to go forth, and you will go
forward in power and might, for no evil can stand before you.

March 6, 2010, Larry Pearson:

A new height is being birthed

An aspect of the stones needs to be cleansed
There is a new assignment
New angels coming
New assignment
New heights
New ground
New sounds
New strength
New frequencies
New graces for new races
Whirlwinds are being released
They will pick up the stones and there will be a cleansing
Stones being put in peoples bellies after they are cleansed in the whirlwind

March 30, 2010 Persis Tiner:[3]

Whirlwinds, whirlwinds; it's coming in the whirlwinds. Be in the rest or you will miss what I am sending. Energy, motion, movement; changing sounds, changing colors; will pass you by in the twinkling of your eye unless your spirit is at rest in Me. Secrets and matter, new and bold, are coming in the whirlwinds as yet untold, and to unfold before your eyes. You will see new shapes and matter, which represent Me.

April 3, 2010, Jana Green:

Deeper still…for the Kingdom of God is not here or there, for the Kingdom is within you. The depth is within you. The expanse of the universe…more to be discovered; more to be uncovered; go for the oil. The treasury is abundant…Go deeper still from the origin to the hereafter. A restoration like never before. It is in the whirlwind, above and below. Back and forth, to and fro, up and down, and here we go. It is the bare elements. The stones undefiled. It is true inheritance. It is an all-consuming fire.

June 3, 2010, Larry Pearson:

New combinations of stones, new expansion, new authority, new ground for a new sound; behold a turn around; behold the full circle. Birthing of a breakthrough. Behold a new thing has come. The old power source has died. A re-wiring and re-firing; a brand new path to be carved out; new levels to occupy in the realms of glory; you've built the foundation but now here comes the rest of the story. Whirlwinds, whirlwinds, whirlwinds; three different levels of whirlwinds...three stages; three breakthroughs; three connections; do not fear, your provision draws near.

July 25, 2010, Larry Pearson:

The platelets are shifting toward righteousness. For no doubt, the King of Righteousness is being revealed. As the King of righteousness is revealed, I will raise up my sons and daughters with righteousness. They are of a new breed; they are of a new seed. As you stand behind this new breed, they will open up a new path, carve out a new path. They will be like the vanguard to pierce like an arrow into that which has exalted itself against the king of righteousness. They will spread out to the east, west, north and south. They will become my new compass. This will be multi-dimensional and multi-purposed. I'm seeing a hurricane-sized whirlwind...what is that Lord? These sons & daughters of righteousness will release a revolution to turn things around, a revolution to bring things full circle, a revolution to open up the timing of the Father, the intention of the Father.

August 3, 2010, Larry Pearson:

Day of His presence; the cloud the size of a man's hand has been. Today I am shifting everything that has been shifted. I am establishing a new order. Pillars of righteousness, pillars of might; behold, the day of the fear of the Lord is at hand. Day of the Kingdom will overshadow the day of the church. Behold, the day of my counsel will supersede and trump the counsel of man...the ungodly hirelings are being displaced. Behold, a birthing of a new move. Behold, the birthing of something completely new. Let My eagles go. Let My eagles come out and fly. Take off the lids, the limits. It has gotten way too politically correct. My Son will be drunk. He will be the God of war in your midst. Behold the day of the righteous. Whirlwinds will blow away the chaff; blow away ungodly roots and shoots.

Behold the realm of the secret place. The day of shaking has come, find your secret place. He that is in you is unshakable. Step into the deep. Come out of the shallow end.

October 5, 2010, Rob Gross:[4]

The gate has opened. The wind is rushing. It is a whirlwind. The army is advancing. The recruits are coming. They are young, but the seeds of greatness are contained within them. The gate is open. I am sending them to you. They will be an advanced tactical training. I am going to release strategy for My end time harvest. The door is opening, but it is not going to stay open forever. It is a season of harvest. Angel of provision. I have seen the need and I shall provide. Fear not. The trumpet is sounding. I am calling my young ones. I am assembling them. Increased authority and power, power—dunamis power…train and send. Train and send. I am going to turn the current on. Get ready for a new season of increase power and authority. Advance, advance, advance. Do not be afraid.

October 19, 2010, Larry Pearson:

Close encounters of the Kingdom Kind. New encounters. Whirlwinds are being released. Be ready to be taken to a new place. You have entered a new ship. It is a ship that is taking you to new quadrants. It will take you awhile to get your footings. Everything is completely new. It will take awhile to get you used to you. It will take you up a notch. There is a whole new realm of rest, dominion and peace. Dominion and peace will produce the provision.

April 18, 2012, Larry Pearson:

A wave of deliverance carried by a wave of My deliverers. New regions of the realms will be delivered, and there will be new treasures and new alliances. There will be a new shaking in the body of Christ. I am releasing whirlwinds to clean out the mess. There are new depths to be revealed, to arise and to bring understanding. New keys to come, greater understanding of the grid and your purpose with the grid, this is a season to focus and hit the mark.

June 15, 2012, Larry Pearson:

I heard, "heavenly realities", heaven's reality being made known. Issues from the Throne, through the Council unto the earth, heaven's reality. Now is the time to see a great divide between the mind of man and the mind of God. The mind of man is going to get more and more twisted, and the mind of God will be brighter and brighter until the Zenith of the perfect day, the day of Christ, the dawning of Christ through a people. The power of agreement will see manifestation and demonstration of heaven's reality and heaven's light for I am He. There's going to be a decree through a body of people, the body and breath of Jesus saying, "I am He". I see the falling over of systems, and robed religious ones falling over as He proclaims with one voice through a people, "I am He". Like the standing up in the spirit in the council of God, earth will see a council on earth standing up, standing up for righteousness, standing up for mercy, and standing up for life. There will be an authority on the standing, like Steven of old, that will be able to proclaim, "Father forgive them for they know not what they do." There will be an unlocking of religion as we know it, and treasures from the religious mountain are going to come forth…You have heard of Him but now you will see Him, and when you see Him, if you position yourself and pray for your friends, there will be something new born through you and many will see and know the council, and the shout of a King will be among them. The shout of the King will be among the authorized council as it is in heaven. Heaven and earth will testify the shout of a king and unearth victory and triumph for an age is passing away and behold a new era is dawning and a whirlwind like a giant tornado will turn, will turn, will turn everything upside right. The wind will begin to blow, and you will begin to know the shout of your King.

September 1, 2013, Larry Pearson:

See a crack, an opening up. This whirlwind will bring transformational understanding. The faces of the sons of the Kingdom are about to shine and dispense a new wine. Get ready to ride the new wave. Position yourself. God is releasing Holy Ghost storm chasers that follow the Cloud, and no longer the crowd. Sonship is about to show up and shake the earth. It is a storm of light, liberty and great joy. New alliances are forming. New connections need to happen. A new shift is taking place, a new breed of worshipping warriors that

EXPLORING HEAVENLY PLACES

will bring upgrade to His Kingdom. Eating scrolls will become the method of transformation.

Amazingly enough these words are only a sampling of all that I have received about the whirlwinds. Finally, I would like to share a word received on August 15, 2013 from Persis Tiner, over a year before my current understanding of the whirlwind. I am awed by the magnitude of what the Lord is doing!

The jump is BIG
BIG, BIG, BIG
Old tent pegs must come OUT
OUT, OUT, OUT

Too big it is to be done alone
I'll send you re-enforcements
Which I have home grown

With the breathe of My wind
Hand in hand with your friends
You'll be propelled
Into regions unknown

This is a BIG one
For this season and time
That I want to reveal
To these friends of mine

As superman
You'll fly into realms yet unknown
Swirling like a dervish
Like dust storms occur
You'll come and you'll go
Into regions both near and far

You'll discover some secrets
Hidden in the winds
You'll unravel some mysteries
Hidden within
You'll deposit My kingdom

Along this new way
As I guide and propel you
For this new day

7

CHAPTER SEVEN

The Lightnings of God

During September 2011, I (Paul) was in Pocatello, Idaho speaking at the Vineyard church. On Saturday evening I taught about spiritual gates, and the connection between gates and healing. At the end of the seminar, a gate appeared and those present walked through it. After everyone had finished I also walked through, but was not at all prepared for what happened next. Suddenly struck by immense power, I ended up on the floor of the church. It felt as if fireworks were being released from the back of my head, and then traveling at great speed to the front of me. I made several efforts to stand up, but it was useless, and power continued to flow for over an hour.

After arriving home, I pondered what had happened and recalled a word by Chuck Pierce that had recently been released through the Elijah List:

> I am sending My lightnings! I have been waiting to fill My children's mouths with the voice of Heaven! I am sending forth My messengers of lightening this hour. I have a people that will become lightning rods! They will then become storms in the earth. You will create storms and you will storm atmospheres of darkness in days ahead.

I am separating the Esaus and Jacobs in your region. That which has warred in your midst as Esau, against My Jacobs, will now change! Lightning is falling on the Jacobs of this hour.

Get ready. You have been activated into the season called 'Lightning'. You have been commissioned to go forth and break open and demonstrate My plan in the season ahead.

I realized that I had experienced 'the lightnings of God', but for what purpose?

In Psalm 18, David cried out to the Lord in his hour of pain and suffering. He was desperate! When would God come to his rescue? The Lord responded in mighty power, riding upon the cherubim as he flew to the aid of David. Then David declared:

The LORD sent out His arrows and scattered the foe, lightnings in abundance.[1]

In Psalm 144, David again spoke of warring against his enemies, and his prayer indicated that his liberation would come with the flashing of lightning:

Bow down Your heavens, O LORD, and come down;
Touch the mountains, and they shall smoke.
Flash forth lightning and scatter them;
Shoot out Your arrows and destroy them.[2]

Soon after returning home from Idaho, Persis Tiner received two prophetic rhymes after reading Chuck Pierce's article, which gave me even more clarity about the lightnings of God:

Storm troopers, forerunners, front guard, spear headers
Timely, piercing
Lightning is capable of bringing change, revelation, judgment and correction

Lightnings and thunderings
Come from above
Piercing the darkness
And bringing My love

Piercing the depths

So dark and so cruel
Setting free captives
And making them bold

Bringing deliverance and healing
To the sick and infirmed
Knocking out power grids
The enemy has formed
And setting free territories
To be free and so bold

Watch now and listen
The thunderings and lightnings to hear
Whether by spirit or
Whether by ear
Whether they be single or
Whether they be many
Appointed by God
To bring freedom to many

The second rhyme came shortly thereafter:

Thunderings and lightnings are just going by
As I sit on my porch
And ponder the sky

Sent from above
By our Father of love
Sent by His hand
For us to understand

The mountains will sing
The valleys will laugh
And angels from heaven will dance much and laugh

New words they shall come
From the lightnings above
Bringing freedom and power
Causing justice and goodness

To move down the streets
Where Satan has been walking with his many feet

The revelation in these happenings
Has yet to be heard
Designed and articulated for those of this hour
Who have been clothed with My great power

As heavenly glories greatly display
A book as it were
From heaven above
Telling the story of My great love

Over the course of several weeks, I continued to discern the lightnings of God. As I was discussing this with a friend from Canada, he mentioned that John D. Lake prophesied that one day in the future the lightnings of God would be released. I wanted to verify that this was true and an Internet search quickly confirmed that the John G. Lake did make such a statement in the 1920's. Here are his words:

> I can see as my spirit discerns the future and reaches out to touch the heart of mankind and the desire of God, that there is coming from heaven a new manifestation of the Holy Spirit in power, and that new manifestation will be in sweetness, in love, in tenderness, and in the power of the Spirit, beyond anything your heart or mind ever saw. The very lightning of God will flash through men's souls. The sons of God will meet the sons of darkness and prevail.[3]

Could it be that we are now in the time of a mighty and fresh release of the power of God that will result in new levels of freedom and healing?

8

CHAPTER EIGHT

Unfolding Revelation of the Lightnings of God

As we've seen, the lightnings of God came to the forefront of our attention in the Fall of 2011, but looking back it's clear that He was speaking about them long before, and He has continued to reveal more and more during the intervening years.

I (Barbara) should not have been surprised (but I was!) when the first instance of lightnings in our accumulated research showed up in association with Mimi Lowe's almost-famous word from August 15, 2005, that launched our *Come Up Higher¹* journey:

> Come up higher
> Come up higher
> You're not high enough yet
> Come up, come up, come up
> Use your power packs—use them
> Open it up
>
> Get the dynamite out

Dynamite your wells
Dynamite your wells
Dynamite your wells
Re-dig your well
Re-dig your well
Re-dig your well

There's your vision
There's your vision
It's been buried too long

As she spoke, another participant saw lightning and declared:

We're going to be birthed into a new realm...the angel's standing with his legs apart in the birthing position...a new plane...We will not come back from this place. The power packs are like thrusters. His lightning is going to thrust you into this place.

The following year, on October 9, 2006, Mimi received another angelic message:

There is a key; a key for you to appropriate
Take hold of this key; take hold of this key
Unlock the treasure that is locked in the second heaven
Pull it down; pull it down
And we will send a lightning bolt a lightning bolt
To go through your bodies
It will go through your bodies
To bring realignment and adjustment
It is my lightning bolt

On March 16, 2007, in an advanced discernment class, Anne Bower[2] declared:

Lightning, lightning! Power, power, power! Lightning, lightning, lightning. This is for each and every one of you; overcoming power, redeeming power, healing power, miracle power, signs and wonder power. It's all available to you. Lightning, lightning, power, power, power; wisdom, wisdom, wisdom, it is available now. Use the power with wisdom; ask and you shall receive. Speak the word. It is power;

it is lightning power. It is the source; speak the word. I've have given you everything you need. You have been equipped, each and every one of you. You are to go out, fully relying on Me. Yes, you will have victory. You will have signs and wonders. I have placed in each one of you, in your heart, this time—now—as to where you are to go, and what you are to do. It is deep in your heart. Some of you will know now, some of you will wait. It is much more than you think, or understand, or seen for this is a new wine. This acts all over again from a new beginning.

Crystal Kain Ross shared transcripts of visions in which Jesus took her into the heavens. Lightning appeared often from 2007 to 2011:

> Far up above us, there were massive enfolding clouds of crimson-gold glory. Lightning bolts were issuing forth constantly from out of the clouds, with pounding sounds and massive reverberations...

> Jesus appeared exceedingly powerful and stately, looking exceptionally grand and regal, and He was dressed in a long white glowing robe, consisting entirely of blinding most-holy light, which had powerful living rays exploding out from it. Each ray was like a miniature bolt of lightning...

> His train was very long, and seemed to never end...it appeared incredibly grand and stately, far greater than I have ever imagined any train to be. It was woven with celestial threads of purest opalescent gossamer living light, and living lightning was very evident...the living light in His train was full of heavenly powerful electric currents, and they sparked and arced as He walked. Each arc sang a little note as it arced, and each was a praise to Him who sits upon the throne... the living lights within the train were always moving and coursing, like the veins in our body, within which our blood flows.

> I was thinking, "Where the Spirit of the Lord is, there is power," and this is so true of the Triune Majesty. I was also aware that this was the same power that was spoken of in the New Testament:

>> *But if the Spirit of Him who raised Jesus from the dead dwells in you, He who raised Christ from the dead will also give life to your mortal*

bodies through His Spirit who dwells in you.³

I knew this to be the same light-filled power that comes down and releases healing and performs miracles, signs and wonders.

The Spirit told me that the speed at which I saw the lightning moving was only as a tiny representation of its actual movement, but it was presented as being much slower because of my present human limitations. If it had not been greatly slowed down, I would not have been able to perceive any of the individual arc's and flows or the beautiful rainbow colors of lightning...Though it was represented as moving slow, it still looked very fast and incredibly powerful. I could hear the electric arcs in the air above the train, coming up out of the lightning veins as the light moved through it. I felt entirely invigorated, as if in hearing and seeing the power in His train, I was now electrified with a portion of His Power through my identification with Him and knowing who He is.

His incredible power and majesty are indescribable, but Elihu did a pretty good job.

> *Hear attentively the thunder of His voice,*
> *And the rumbling that comes from His mouth.*
> *He sends it forth under the whole heaven,*
> *His lightning to the ends of the earth.*
> *After it a voice roars;*
> *He thunders with His majestic voice,*
> *And He does not restrain them when His voice is heard.⁴*

[In another vision] Jesus turned around on His War horse and began riding very fast on ahead of us...we began to ride very fast too as we followed Him...He then commanded us, "Encircle the enemy, now. Speak and shout, warriors of My living light! The time has come for Victory! Shout, for the Battle belongs to Us!"

At this command, we encircled the demon forces and we all began to shout. The sound was so loud that it began to cause many of the evil demons to fall down, completely paralyzed by the sound... When the words were voiced, they came out very fast and each one quickly seemed to gather momentum and turn into a lightning bolts of power, which went on to strike their targets. Each word lightning bolt seemed to be like a heat-seeking scud missile, although it was not a scud missile but a demon-seeking missile…and as this was happening Jesus was participating too. There were words coming from His mouth, and all His words were holy and living, and laced with living fire…His word lightning bolts came down from above and joined with ours. When they did, each of our lightning word bolts then took on even greater, exponential power, becoming an immeasurable striking force. It was completely inescapable and unlimited in power when His strength was added. Never before has my understanding of the Bible reference to a two-edged sword in his mouth been so clear; and with it, He strikes.

[On another occasion] Jesus then turned me to Him and touched my eyes with His fingers. When He did it was like bolts of lightning laced with electricity shot into me, yet I was not destroyed.

In 2010, the prophetic words about lightning continued. From Lewis Crompton,[5] on July 19, 2010:

Come into My plumb line
There you will receive a sign
The victory is divine
You cannot win by yourself
You can only win with Me
Take yourself off the shelf
I am not done with thee
For that which is old I am making new
For where there was no resolution I am bringing resolution
Where there was darkness I am bringing light
Where there was evil I am bringing My presence
You are light in darkness designed to shine
How will you fight the darkness if you do not have the light?
For the rod on your back is a lightning rod
It connects to My power, to My suddenlies

During 2010, Raylene Zendejas[6] had a series of visions over several months in which she saw the Lord's army approaching Aslan's Place to do battle, and when it finally arrived there was a big spiritual breakthrough. She sent updates to Paul as she watched the army advance in visions:

> I keep seeing the Army that the Lord is sending to us advancing…
> it is an awesome and very large Army. Their feet are very loud, and
> as they come it is getting louder. There is thunder and lightning in
> front of them and the battle is intense all around them…

> This morning I had a clear vision of the approaching army…There
> is lightning flashing in front of the army and it seems to be in a
> mist of clouds or a veil of sorts…At moments there were clearings
> of the mist so that I could see portions of the Army. I could see
> banners and long streamer-looking flags whirling as they advanced.
> They were deep royal colors: purple, blue, red and gold. There is a
> lot of flashing from within the army; bright brilliant flashing (almost
> translucent gold and white light)…it was an overwhelming sight! Joy
> filled my heart as I watched but it was a different kind of joy that I
> have never experienced before. It kind of felt like joy mixed with a
> deep peace and a sense of being complete.

November 14, 2010, Jana Green:

> There is a place of inheritance that my people have not yet known.
> It is in the depths of Me, Elohim. It is My vindication that you are
> redeemed. Have you heard the roar of My voice in the thunder?
> Have you seen the flashing of lighting in the clouds and wondered?
> Now watch and see, the mature man will look just like Me…Don't be
> dismayed, for I have overcome the world. You have been realigned
> and redefined for it is just about time for the millennium reign to be
> revealed…

February 21, 2012, Jana Green:

> Possess the gates; remove the janitor
> Collapse the walls; your enemy will be scattered
> Watch the paths and ride the light
> The lightnings of God will give you flight
> You are more connected than you know
> Gate to gate is where wisdom calls
> So don't harden your hearts when you hear His voice

He passed through the heavens so you may have a choice
Eternal rest that is where there are many rooms
The word of the Lord will bring you through
Freedom for the oppressed, freedom for the upright, freedom for
the captive
For there is nothing hidden from His sight.
It is a sound of creation, a sound of renewal
Depression will flee
This is true revival

September 2012, a participant in an Intern Week:

Remember your main purpose here on earth is to be a lightning
rod—a vessel to hold the Light of God—the power of God—to
bring not only yourself, but also others to the light—so they too
can become lightning rods—a vessel that can hold and disperse the
powerful Love of God.

In a Biblical Discernment and Exploration session on October 27, 2012, after
dealing with an evil gate, Paul began discerning lightning:

What I feel now is the lightnings of God as a sharp pain in my head,
and there have now been three lightnings...I feel many lightnings
now. Let's look at Psalm 18:4-7:

> The pangs of death surrounded me,
> And the floods of ungodliness made me afraid.
> The sorrows of Sheol surrounded me;
> The snares of death confronted me.
> In my distress I called upon the LORD,
> And cried out to my God;
> He heard my voice from His temple,
> And my cry came before Him, even to His ears.
> Then the earth shook and trembled;
> The foundations of the hills also quaked and were shaken,
> Because He was angry.

The sorrows of Sheol are in the depth, the ungodly depth. Now look at verse 13-14:

The LORD thundered from heaven,
And the Most High uttered His voice,
Hailstones and coals of fire.
He sent out His arrows and scattered the foe,
Lightnings in abundance, and He vanquished them.

I feel like that's what is happening right now—the Lord is coming as lightning and destroying the enemy. So, Lord Jesus, we all now come in agreement, and we take our sword and come against the enemy in the power of our unity and under your authority. Okay now I have a sense that we all can walk through this gate, and I feel this is a place of healing.

July 2014, from Larry Pearson:

Have you heard the news today? Have you heard the news today? The news of Yahweh. Your gaze has been trapped; it's been trapped in news of the world…Have you heard the news today? Angels on assignment, and there are new ones coming that are a whole lot bigger than before. There are myriads coming, coming to push you forward. Myriads of angelic hosts and living creatures are coming like a massive army to push this forward…they will push you and stretch your head, and pull your head out of the unholy news. If you choose, for you will be an epistle of kingdom news…Satellites shall blaze with the lightnings of God, and lightnings of the good news for myriads of angles and living creatures; and wild, wild, wild, be-ings with thousands of eyes are here to draw near and carry you into a higher seer realm that will scare the hell out of the region.

The words and experiences detailed above are confirmed over and over again in scripture:

The LORD thundered from heaven,
And the Most High uttered His voice.
He sent out arrows and scattered them;
Lightning bolts, and He vanquished them.[7]

The voice of Your thunder was in the whirlwind; The lightnings lit up the world; The earth trembled and shook.[8]

A fire goes before Him,
And burns up His enemies round about.
His lightnings light the world;
The earth sees and trembles.[9]

The chariots rage in the streets,
They jostle one another in the broad roads;
They seem like torches,
They run like lightning.[10]

Then the LORD will be seen over them,
And His arrow will go forth like lightning.
The LORD GOD will blow the trumpet,
And go with whirlwinds from the south.[11]

When He utters His voice, There is a multitude of waters in the heavens: "And He causes the vapors to ascend from the ends of the earth. He makes lightning for the rain, He brings the wind out of His treasuries." [12]

Writing about entering the rest of God, Paul spoke of the cherubs as mentioned in Ezekiel and Revelation:

So, visualize the four of them somehow all going forward and moving together in unity with the fire in their feet. I believe this is where the anointing comes from. Of course, the anointing actually comes from the Holy Spirit, but it appears that the living creatures have between their feet the fire that sometimes hits us as we worship. It also appears as lightning—pretty spectacular!

Then I looked, and behold, a whirlwind was coming out of the north, a great cloud with raging fire engulfing itself; and brightness was all around it and radiating out of its midst like the color of amber, out of the midst of the fire. Also from within it came the likeness of four living creatures. And this was their appearance: they had the likeness of a man. Each one had four faces, and each one had four wings... Their wings touched one another. The creatures did not turn when they went, but each one went straight forward...And each one went straight forward; they went wherever the spirit wanted to go, and they did not turn when they went. As for the likeness of the living creatures, their appearance was like burning coals of fire, like the appearance of torches going back and forth among the living creatures. The fire was bright, and out of the fire went lightning. And the living creatures ran back and forth, in appearance like a flash of lightning.[13]

Looking back at all of the words, experiences and scriptures, it's interesting to realize that our common understanding of lightning from an earthly perspective fits the heavenly version perfectly. As a noun, a very simple definition of lightning is that it's an electrical discharge of very short duration and high voltage between a cloud and the ground or within a cloud, accompanied by a bright flash, and usually thunder. As an adjective, lightning is something that is very quick. Even simpler, the meaning boils down to light, speed and power, and as magnificent as physical lightning storms may appear, they pale in comparison to God's lightnings.

At the end of the previous chapter Paul asked the question, "Could it be that we are now in the time of a mighty and fresh release of the power of God that will result in new levels of freedom and healing?" The answer so far certainly appears to be yes.

9

CHAPTER NINE
Introduction to Clouds

Clouds—so amorphous, with no definite form or shape. From brilliant white to thunderous black; fluffy, feathery, or flat; translucent or dense; towering or tiny; the descriptions are endless. Many of us have contrasting cloud memories; pleasant lazy childhood days spent cloud gazing in awe at one that looks just like a dog or cat or bear; versus horrifying, humongous, dark funnel clouds, bearing down toward the ground and threatening to wipe out everything in their path. Personally, I (Barbara) am intrigued by the view from a plane as, looking down at a vast, white, and seemingly solid carpet, I ponder how it would feel if it were possible to get out and walk. There can be no doubt of God's creativity as we observe clouds:

> *Now it happened in the meantime that the sky became black with clouds and wind, and there was a heavy rain.*[1]

> *He binds up the water in His thick clouds,*
> *Yet the clouds are not broken under it.*
> *He covers the face of His throne,*
> *And spreads His cloud over it.*[2]

Look to the heavens and see;
And behold the clouds—
They are higher than you.[3]

Listen to this, O Job;
Stand still and consider the wondrous works of God.
Do you know when God dispatches them,
And causes the light of His cloud to shine?
Do you know how the clouds are balanced,
Those wondrous works of Him who is perfect in knowledge?[4]

The clouds poured out water;[5]

Who covers the heavens with clouds,[6]

Apparently, God loves His cloud creations, for He surrounds Himself with them:

And the LORD went before them by day in a pillar of cloud to lead them along
the way, and by night in a pillar of fire to give them light, that they might travel
by day and by night.[7]
He bowed the heavens also, and came down
With darkness under His feet.
He rode upon a cherub, and flew;
And He was seen upon the wings of the wind.
He made darkness canopies around Him,
Dark waters and thick clouds of the skies.
From the brightness before Him
Coals of fire were kindled.[8]

Thick clouds cover Him…[9]

Clouds and darkness surround Him…[10]

He made darkness His secret place;
His canopy around Him was dark waters
And thick clouds of the skies.[11]

He lays the beams of His upper chambers in the waters,
Who makes the clouds His chariot,
Who walks on the wings of the wind...[12]

Clouds may hold either tremendous promise or the threat of terrible danger, depending on whether of not on is a child of God:

For the day is near,
Even the day of the LORD is near;
It will be a day of clouds, the time of the Gentiles.[13]

For the day of the LORD is coming,
For it is at hand:
A day of darkness and gloominess,
A day of clouds and thick darkness,
Like the morning clouds spread over the mountains.[14]

That day is a day of wrath,
A day of trouble and distress,
A day of devastation and desolation,
A day of darkness and gloominess,
A day of clouds and thick darkness,[15]

Like the appearance of a rainbow in a cloud on a rainy day, so was the appearance of the brightness all around it. This was the appearance of the likeness of the glory of the LORD.[16]

Then the sign of the Son of Man will appear in heaven, and then all the tribes of the earth will mourn, and they will see the Son of Man coming on the clouds of heaven with power and great glory.[17]

In October 2013, during a Come Up Higher conference in New Jersey, Melchizedek revealed Himself. Paul spent some time teaching and helping those who were present to discern Melchizedek. They continued to sense Him interceding so they waited for a period of time until Paul discerned that they had been taken to the Ancient of Days court. He started reading Daniel 7 and, coming to verse 13, which is about the Son of Man being presented to the Ancient of Days, he realized something new. It says that they brought Him to the Ancient of Days, 'they' being the clouds that are spiritual beings.

I was watching in the night visions,
And behold, One like the Son of Man,
Coming with the clouds of heaven!
He came to the Ancient of Days,
And they brought Him near before Him.

Next, Paul did a search for previous prophetic words that contained something about clouds and was surprised at how many words there were. Then, when he asked the Lord how many clouds there were he had a sense of trillions. Also, he sensed that the clouds seemed tied to the whirlwinds, which we found had been the case during a meeting in March 2009:

(Mimi Lowe) Whirlwind of fire, whirlwind of fire, whirlwind of fire; expand, expand, expand, expand; you've never been here before. Shifting sands, shifting sands, shifting sands; Chariots of fire, chariots of fire, chariots of fire to take you higher; come on board. Take you higher; explore other dimensions.

(Paul Cox) The whole room is going up.

(Participant) I can see all kinds of clouds below. The clouds seem colored; they are not white clouds. They are a kind of yellow. I see a ridge of clouds. I keep going higher still. We are going forward. All I can do is to say what I am seeing. It is like being in another world. I can see we are above mountains full of forests. We've gone over the clouds.

During an advanced discernment session in May 2010, Larry Pearson spoke these words.

New whirlwinds, new clouds; these clouds are full of God's substance, a release of angels, ministers of the heirs of salvation...for Aslan's Place. Now ask the Lord for wisdom to know how to ask for Him to dispatch the angels where they need to go...

This is now the hour of the Order of Melchizedek to execute the will of God, to ask for the release of dispatching the angels of God, spiritual beings, living creatures. Decree a thing and it will be. A new authority, a new authority is coming on Aslan's Place, on Joel's well, on the prayer ministers. A shift has come, a new level of glory…

As we are going up, we are coming through clouds. We are busting through clouds, ungodly energies and ungodly lies of who we were. Now is coming forth a new identity of pure gold, the divine nature, the nature of divine light with which we are one.

During the latter part of 2010, when Raylene Zendejas experienced her ongoing vision of an angelic army approaching Aslan's Place from the southwest, one of her email updates to Paul indicated that clouds encompassed it:

There is lightning flashing in front of the army, and it seems to be in a mist of clouds, or a veil of sorts. Flying out in front of the army is a massive, totally white eagle that is fiercely looking from east to west, screeching as it flies forward.

During a session of biblical exploration in October 2012, Paul recalled a prayer session in which he didn't know what to do next and he thought, "Jesus, you need to come as the Son of Man." Immediately, he recalled the Matthew 26:64:

Jesus said to him, "It is as you said. Nevertheless, I say to you, hereafter you will see the Son of Man sitting at the right hand of the Power, and coming on the clouds of heaven."

Soon, Paul realized that the group gathered at Aslan's Place for the session was also seated in the midst of the cloud of witnesses:

Therefore we also, since we are surrounded by so great a cloud of witnesses, let us lay aside every weight, and the sin which so easily ensnares us, and let us run with endurance the race that is set before us, looking unto Jesus, the author and finisher of our faith, who for the joy that was set before Him endured the cross, despising the shame, and has sat down at the right hand of the throne of God.[18]

As the discussion continued, there was a reference to the end-time harvest and another scripture was read that speaks of Jesus coming on the clouds:

Then I looked, and behold, a white cloud, and on the cloud sat One like the Son of Man, having on His head a golden crown, and in His hand a sharp sickle. And another angel came out of the temple, crying with a loud voice to

Him who sat on the cloud, "Thrust in Your sickle and reap, for the time has come for You to reap, for the harvest of the earth is ripe." So He who sat on the cloud thrust in His sickle on the earth, and the earth was reaped.[19]

In the context of a long prophetic word about the revelation of the sons of God in November 2012, Lewis Crompton spoke of, "clouds of reckoning, clouds of redeeming."

On December 9, 2012, Crystal Kain Ross received a word of judgment regarding a situation that is not relevant here, but the references to winds and clouds is:

A hot wind, from the bare heights in the wilderness comes at My command…not a wind to fan or cleanse from chaff, as when threshing, but a wind too strong and full for winnowing, comes…I will also speak in judgment against My people. Behold, the enemy's clouds have come up (from the pit); his chariots like the whirlwind; his horses are swifter than eagles.

10

CHAPTER TEN

Unfolding Revelation of Clouds

During a youth group in May 2013, Larry Pearson heard:

> He's releasing the billows of his presence
> He's establishing pillars all over the earth
> Pillars of fire and clouds of his presence
> For a shift has come
> And a new thing has begun...

August 18, 2013, in Collingwood, Canada, Larry Pearson received a message from an elemental spirit:

> And when they come and have common passion, you will have a sound and you will be a sound, mmmmmmmm (Larry humming). With a mere sound, cities will be delivered; people groups will be delivered. The majesty of the Kingdom is in the sound. Find your sound. The gates are opening. The gates are opening...(Larry singing)...your King is coming in the clouds of glory. Coming on the clouds of Glory. The uncontaminated elements will now lift you and carry you through the King's gate...(more humming)...the sound of

dominion, the sound of dominion. I'm tuning you to a sound of dominion, calibration to His dominion, attuning desire and dominion...whirlwinds in the glory...

So, now we're back to October 2013, and Paul's revelation about clouds being spiritual beings. A participant, standing in a cloud, was waiting on the Lord when she heard:

Acceleration of time. I'm taking back time, the time that has been lost in your lives. Releasing, releasing that acceleration through the clouds. I'm sending it in the clouds, My transport to send forward the acceleration.

I'm releasing My whirlwind. I'm releasing the whirlwind through the clouds to uproot, overthrow, tear down, and destroy everything unrighteous...through the clouds. It's My whirlwind that's coming. It's My whirlwind that's coming.

There's fire, wind, and rain in the clouds...and sound...My word comes forth in the clouds. My Word comes forth in the clouds. My voice is heard through the clouds. They transmit My voice to be heard. It's the sound of thunder, the sound of thunder to cleanse. I'm releasing My voice in the cloud. The audible voice of the Lord is coming to you in the cloud. You will hear me louderrrr. You will hear me louderrrrr. Wake up and strengthen yourselves; wake up and strengthen yourselves; wake up and strengthen yourselves!

As she was speaking, another participant was also getting a prophetic word:

Paul said earlier that we are in the battle of ages and it seems the enemy is winning. I used to be in the Marines and we would get deliveries when we ran out of supplies on the front lines. What God is doing in these last days for this great battle, is releasing the clouds as our supply source--as much as we're willing to carry, as much as we are willing to receive, all that we need in the form of power, anointing, resources, food—physically as well as spiritually. Whatever we need as far as wisdom and knowledge He will supply in abundance.

I also saw that the clouds were delivering these supplies with a detonator so that we will be at the right place at the right time, and when all the unrighteous power is overwhelming us, it will be just like Hiroshima, obliterated in a split second by the Power of God. It will be just like when Jesus was in the Garden of Gethsemane. He said "I Am He," and all the soldiers fell down. All the power we need to overcome is going to be delivered right to our door like FedEx, so now know that there is not going to be a delay for delivery for victory, it will be real time, for all those who want to walk in His anointing power and mission.

The following month, November 2013, in a webinar exploration session with Paul Knight[1] and other members of Aslan's Place, London, Paul read Isaiah 54:16:

Behold, I have created the blacksmith
Who blows the coals in the fire,
Who brings forth an instrument for his work;
And I have created the spoiler to destroy.

Paul explained:

Another word for blacksmith is 'craftsman' or 'engraver,' and I can discern the Engraver on my head. Where the NKJV says 'spoiler,' the word is actually 'destroyer,' and I can also feel Destroyer, who is a righteous spiritual being. Initially, I wasn't sure if these are two different beings but my thinking now, and it was confirmed last night, is that this is sort of a dimensional being that has two sides. One is the Engraver, and the other is the Destroyer. Now, notice this! After the Destroyer and Engraver are released then we have the promise of verse 17:

No weapon formed against you shall prosper,
And every tongue which rises against you in judgment
You shall condemn.
This is the heritage of the servants of the LORD,
And their righteousness is from Me,"
Says the LORD.

As the session continued, Lewis Crompton spoke this word, observing that the cloud felt like it was releasing itself once the words were given:

> How will you reap without the harvest?
> How will you harvest without growth?
> How will you grow without the rain?
> How will it rain without the clouds?
> There is no harvest without the rain
> Let me reign (rain)
> My word will not return void

Isaiah 55:10-13 was then read:

> *For as the rain comes down, and the snow from heaven,*
> *And do not return there,*
> *But water the earth,*
> *And make it bring forth and bud,*
> *That it may give seed to the sower And bread to the eater,*
> *So shall My word be that goes forth from My mouth;*
> *It shall not return to Me void,*
> *But it shall accomplish what I please,*
> *And it shall prosper in the thing for which I sent it.*
> *For you shall go out with joy,*
> *And be led out with peace;*
> *The mountains and the hills,*
> *Shall break forth into singing before you,*
> *And all the trees of the field shall clap their hands.*
> *Instead of the thorn shall come up the cypress tree,*
> *And instead of the brier shall come up the myrtle tree;*
> *And it shall be to the LORD for a name,*
> *For an everlasting sign that shall not be cut off.*

The discussion continued:

(Paul Cox) Do our praise or agreement or words become clouds, and because they are an agreement with Jesus, the clouds then send forth the rain that accomplishes His purposes? Is our agreement with Him that forms these living beings called clouds that then respond?

(Paul Knight) Well, that goes with the proverb that says, "Life and death is in the tongue." If we are speaking death, then there'll be death; but if we are speaking life, that's going to be in agreement with Him.

(Paul Cox) It gives a whole new meaning to it, doesn't it?

(Paul Knight) Yes, it makes you wonder every time you open your mouth!

(Paul Cox) Exactly.

(Stephen G) In the natural, it is water that gives you life.

(Paul Knight) And doesn't it say that when we go before the throne that all our words will be judged, and if all our words are in a cloud???

(Emma C) It says 'the Cloud of witnesses' doesn't it?

(Paul Cox) Yes that's right, and then you wonder if there is some more meaning to 'the cloud of witnesses' than we have understood. There's so much more than this!

Afterward, Paul summarized for his notes:

During the session I felt the glorious ones, but they were contaminated. I then read Jude, remembered the clouds, and felt that words were droplets that made up clouds. Jude 10-13 speaks both of evil clouds that are filled with water, and of evil words:

> But these speak evil of whatever they do not know; and whatever they know naturally, like brute beasts, in these things they corrupt themselves. Woe to them! For they have gone in the way of Cain, have run greedily in the error of Balaam for profit, and perished in the rebellion of Korah. These are spots in your love feasts, while they feast with you without fear, serving only themselves. They are clouds without water, carried about by the winds; late autumn trees without fruit, twice dead, pulled up by the roots; raging waves of the sea, foaming up their own shame; wandering stars for whom is reserved the blackness of darkness forever.

In June 2014, at a meeting at Niagara on the Lake in Canada, Larry Pearson received the word:

> Hey, hey, awake your trumpeters. It's time for the trumpeters of the covenant to awaken. We are here to awaken covenant power. Covenant power for the hour, to establish the showers; the showers of new seasons, new reasons, it will feel like Christmas in July! For the showering of my presence will be upon you. Take heed what you hear. For the measure that you hear, it will make you fear. Hey, get your head out of the wrong cloud; your head has been in the wrong cloud. You're leaning on understanding that is not God. It's time for the head of the church to emerge, and rest, on a body that is headless.

> Unless we become headless of our own understanding, His head and headship will be disconnected, despondent, and will not function. The body needs the Head. So awake oh trumpeters! Awake! Awake in Zion! Come up the mountain of the Lord. Come up, and I will teach you My ways to see, My ways. Get unplugged, so the realms can see you. The realms are seeing what they've deposited on you, but it isn't you. Its time for the unveiling of who Father says you are, blameless and holy, a spotless bride that lives by His side. We will be like the cloud removal company. We've been assigned to burst your bubble so the authentic you will emerge and build in partnership with edification, habitation and transformation.

Moving along to February 2015, we were at an Aslan's Place summit when we were taken in the Spirit to the Ancient of Days court. One of the men in the room was surrounded by an ungodly cloud, which was the result of things people had said or thought about him, or that he'd said or thought about himself. Paul advised him that the unrighteous clouds can be removed simply by saying, "I do not receive that." Then, after reviewing some of the information already presented, he concluded:

> Every word that we think or say is a drip—a drop of water from a cloud. Jesus will come with the clouds, on the clouds. It is our worship, witness and testimony that present the Son of Man to the Father. We all agree that He is the Son of God.

> You cannot be put into a bad place unless you come into agreement

with ungodly words. We want our clouds to be full of praise and worship and righteousness so that we will correctly present the Son to the Ancient of Days.

As we consider the effect that words may have had on us, we can pray:

Lord Jesus, I repent for all the words and thoughts I've had against myself. Lord, please break the power of all words spoken against me. I want to be in the cloud of your glory.

11

CHAPTER ELEVEN
The Clouds of Witnesses

Immediately following Hebrews 11, the Faith Hall of Fame, we are encouraged in our own race of faith:

> *Therefore we also, since we are surrounded by so great a cloud of witnesses, let us lay aside every weight, and the sin which so easily ensnares us, and let us run with endurance the race that is set before us, looking unto Jesus, the author and finisher of our faith, who for the joy that was set before Him endured the cross, despising the shame, and has sat down at the right hand of the throne of God.*[1]

Though this is the only direct biblical reference to the cloud of witnesses, we've already seen in the discussion of how our words relate to the clouds that there may be more meaning to the cloud of witnesses than we have previously understood.

I (Barbara) had a dream in February 2008, which involved the cloud of witnesses:

> I was initially with a woman (represents the church), and we were in a hallway outside a big sports arena. We could see a couple of teams

in separate rooms preparing for the upcoming game. The woman and I parted, planning to meet up again later, and I walked through an entrance to the floor of the arena that was familiar and I knew I'd been through it before. However, I soon encountered barriers to the actual playing floor. It had just been refinished, but was now dry, except for being a little sticky around the edges. A referee, who I believe was an angel, approached me and said I wasn't supposed to go this way, but allowed me to walk across the highly polished floor to a side door because I could not be allowed to go back the way I'd come. As I walked across the soon-to-be-used playing floor, I looked up and saw that every seat was full of absolutely silent spectators, and it was a huge crowd, but I was not at all embarrassed.

After waking up, I recorded my impressions of what the dream meant:

This seems like something that is taking place in front of the great cloud of witnesses. Perhaps this is a message that the church is in preparation for the main event. The time for action is almost here. I have been allowed to see this, but why? To encourage the church? Is this the time of the seventh seal when there is silence in heaven?[2] The sense that I had been there before and that there could be no return to the past was very strong.

In August 2008, Paul described in a ministry school how he discerns the cloud of witnesses. Amidst the subsequent discussion, there was a prophetic word from Mimi Lowe, as well as more insights from Paul and some prayers:

(Paul) This is the cloud of witnesses. It feels like an amphitheater on my head. We're at the bottom of the cloud of witnesses.

(Mimi) This is the heavenly council. This is the heavenly council. This is the heavenly council where the cloud of witnesses is. What do you have to say? What do you have to say? What are your complaints? What do you want to bring to me? What do you want to bring to me? Come, come, let us reason together. This is the time. This is the time. Let us reason together. Share with me your heart; your heart's complaints. Share with me your grievances. And let justice be rendered, let justice be rendered; justice, this is the time for justice, justice, justice. This is your hour. This is your moment;

this is your day. The enemy is at the sideline. They are waiting; they are waiting for judgment to be rendered. And I will speak on your behalf. I will speak on your behalf. I am your advocate. But you must come to me. Talk to me. Share with me. Come, let us reason together.

(Paul) There's an invitation to issue your complaint before the Lord. What is it that you want? Where has there been injustice in your life? This is His invitation, not mine. Jesus is inviting you now, and promises that He will be our advocate before the father at this point. This is the moment, our hour, and our day. What is your complaint?

(Paul prays and participants agree) Lord, summon the enemy who has accused us, coming against us and our family line, personally, all those that have warred against us in every facet of our lives. To this council you will summon the enemy. Jesus is our advocate, we ask you to appeal to the father to have justice, rendered to us because the blood of Jesus was shed on the cross for our sins. Lord you issue the verdict to the enemy. We ask you to contend against those who contend against us.

(Paul comments) I feel a massive amount of evil, churning, agitated. I feel beings that brought much pain to you, your family, your life, my life, my family; sorrow and sadness; emotional and financial distress. Will not the Judge of Heaven do right?

(Paul prays) Lord, we declare You will do right; that you will decide favorably upon us that were redeemed by your blood.

Lord, we declare that we want to represent You as a victorious people, as an example to the people of the earth of Your church that is healthy, and whole, and victorious. Lord, we declare we're tired of being the victims. We want to assume our positions as the revealed sons of God on the earth. We want to walk in our sonship, and in our position as those that have stewardship of Your creation. We ask for Your power to flow through us so that we walk in that position, for we understand it's not by our power or our might, but by Your Spirit that we can do this. Our desire is to give all glory to You. Arise, oh God, and defeat your enemies.

Lord, we feel the enemy has tried to wear us down; many of us feel worn down, worn out from the battle. Your word says the enemy tries to wear down the saints and Lord, we feel like that. We declare it's time for us to be Your victorious church. It's time for us to cause the enemy to tremble rather than the other way around.

(Paul comments) I feel prayers coming down in the Spirit of God. The Spirit is prompting us to pray.

(Participant offers a prophetic word) The blood of all the martyrs, the cloud of witnesses that went before us, and what they died for. Now the book is ready to be opened, the book of Daniel, because everything they had, everything they died for, every part is ready to be released into the body, and we will get what they spilled their blood for. They will watch, they will have the redemption, and they will see you go forward. They will see you take up those swords in battle. It's what they died for, and they're standing there, watching and waiting. Father we thank you for what they did and what they stood for.

On many occasions over the years, the presence of the cloud of witnesses has been discerned, especially in times of spiritual triumph. Sometimes they are simply observing, but when all has been said and done, they are frequently cheering, as in this word from 2012:

The cloud of witnesses and the saints; the redeemed, the righteous ones made perfect; the cloud of witnesses are cheering for us as for troops going to war. We are in the arena; we are in the center, in the front, with the troops are lined up behind us. As in Hebrews 12:4, we are surrounded by the Cloud of Witnesses.

As we consider the cloud of witnesses, it is appropriate to remember the glorious company of which we are a part:

For you have not come to the mountain that may be touched and that burned with fire, and to blackness and darkness and tempest, and the sound of a trumpet and the voice of words, so that those who heard it begged that the word should not be spoken to them anymore. (For they could not endure what was commanded: "And if so much as a beast touches the mountain, it shall be stoned or shot with an arrow." And so terrifying was the sight that Moses said, "I am exceedingly afraid and trembling.") But you have come to Mount Zion and to the city of the living God, the heavenly Jerusalem, to an innumerable company of angels, to the general assembly and church of the firstborn who are registered in heaven, to God the Judge of all, to the spirits of just men made perfect, to Jesus the Mediator of the new covenant, and to the blood of sprinkling that speaks better things than that of Abel.[3]

12

CHAPTER TWELVE
The Rain

According to God's perfect weather pattern, after the clouds come the rain, as referenced already in a number of prophetic words. What more can we learn about rain from the Bible? For one thing, it's easy to see that throughout God's word, rain could indicate either a promised blessing or a threatened curse. It may also have been used as a prophetic indication of God's power.

During the years from creation to the flood, rain did not exist on earth and a mist watered the ground:

> *This is the history of the heavens and the earth when they were created, in the day that the LORD God made the earth and the heavens, before any plant of the field was in the earth and before any herb of the field had grown. For the LORD God had not caused it to rain on the earth, and there was no man to till the ground; but a mist went up from the earth and watered the whole face of the ground.*[1]

Should we be surprised by the skepticism of the already-unbelieving people when Noah came along, building a huge ark and prophesying that God would cause rain to fall and cover the earth? And so the rain, such a familiar aspect of our weather today, first appeared as judgment upon the sinful depths of depravity to which mankind had descended:

> *For after seven more days I will cause it to rain on the earth forty days and forty nights, and I will destroy from the face of the earth all living things that I have made.*[2]

> *And the rain was on the earth forty days and forty nights.*[3]

Conversely, post-flood, God would also withhold rain as a judgment, resulting in terrible droughts. As this is written, California is enduring a record-breaking drought. Is this a sign of God's displeasure? I wouldn't be surprised, for much of our good and highly productive farmlands now lie barren, dustbowls producing nothing but tumbleweeds:

> *Take heed to yourselves, lest your heart be deceived, and you turn aside and serve other gods and worship them, lest the LORD's anger be aroused against you, and He shut up the heavens so that there be no rain, and the land yield no produce, and you perish quickly from the good land which the LORD is giving you.*[4]

Rain is often seen as a blessing for the faithful, and is evidence of the goodness of God:

> *If you walk in My statutes and keep My commandments, and perform them, then I will give you rain in its season, the land shall yield its produce, and the trees of the field shall yield their fruit.*[5]

> *The LORD will open to you His good treasure, the heavens, to give the rain to your land in its season, and to bless all the work of your hand. You shall lend to many nations, but you shall not borrow.*[6]

> *Give ear, O heavens, and I will speak;*
> *And hear, O earth, the words of my mouth.*
> *Let my teaching drop as the rain,*
> *My speech distill as the dew,*
> *As raindrops on the tender herb,*
> *And as showers on the grass.*
> *For I proclaim the name of the LORD:*
> *Ascribe greatness to our God.*[7]

Rain down, you heavens, from above,
And let the skies pour down righteousness;
Let the earth open, let them bring forth salvation,
And let righteousness spring up together.
I, the LORD, have created it.[8]

As a prophetic sign, rain draws attention toward God. In October 2014, during a time of unfolding revelation in Hawaii, an underlying drama was taking place, as the approaching Hurricane Anna appeared to be increasing in strength. It seemed that a major catastrophe was imminent but as the storm slowly approached, it began drifting away from the islands. When Paul preached on Sunday morning, people were overcome by the prophetic nature of what was happening because Anna means grace. To review, a hurricane is a whirlwind that moves in a counter clockwise direction and brings destructive power, but the effect of this hurricane was a wonderfully gentle rain, evidence of His grace.

More recently, in July 2015, the tail end of Hurricane Dolores moved through southern California, bringing some very unusual rain along with it. I (Barbara) live near the coast and Paul lives about 1½ hour away, up in the high desert; and it just doesn't rain in July in either location! But rain it did, and relaxing on my patio in the wonderful coolness that followed an unexpected downpour, I received a call from Paul. Excited, he wanted to tell me about the gentle rain that was now falling on his home—a rain very similar to that which he'd experienced in Hawaii. But this rain wasn't about grace, for Delores means sorrows, and Paul sensed that it was a prophetic picture of God's tears of sorrow over the sinful compromise within His church.

> *"Is today not the wheat harvest? I will call to the LORD, and He will send thunder and rain, that you may perceive and see that your wickedness is great, which you have done in the sight of the LORD, in asking a king for yourselves." So Samuel called to the LORD, and the LORD sent thunder and rain that day; and all the people greatly feared the LORD and Samuel.[9]*

There are times when spiritual rain manifests in the powerful presence of God, unseen and unfelt by some, but very evident to those who discern it. A short excerpt from a conversation in a meeting in October 2012, illustrates this:

(Jana Green) I'm getting drenched.

(Paul) Oh, Ken said he felt he was in the snow. That's right, the cold of course! (FYI, Paul is not a fan of cold weather!)

(Jana) Well, you know every time the Lord comes up against the enemies of Israel in the Old Testament it's always with hail or snow. So whenever I feel cold, there is a deliverance happening a lot of the time.

(Paul) That's true, isn't it!

(Jana) It was snowing in Zalmon when He came against the kings.

(Paul) Say again.

(Jana) It was snowing in Zalmon—Psalm 68:

> *O God, when You went out before Your people,*
> *When You marched through the wilderness, Selah*
> *The earth shook;*
> *The heavens also dropped rain at the presence of God;*
> *Sinai itself was moved at the presence of God, the God of Israel.*
> *You, O God, sent a plentiful rain,*
> *Whereby You confirmed Your inheritance,*
> *When it was weary.*
>
> *When the Almighty scattered kings in it,*
> *It was white as snow in Zalmon.*[10]

My mother experienced this manifestation of God's power on her death-bed in 2014, and it was an encounter that astounded her and encouraged those of us who were privileged to observe it. She had already encountered the Lord earlier in the day in a miraculous way when He delivered her from a multitude of concerns that had been weighing her down, and entering into a time of anointed worship such as she'd never before experienced. She was so full of the Spirit that her dull-and-almost-lifeless-appearing brown eyes were transformed into beautiful, shining beacons of His light. But eventually she tired, and decided it was time for a nap. When she awakened a few hours later, I was reminded of a picture I have of my son as a baby; staring at his hand the first time he realized it was attached. That same astonished look was on Mom's face as she gazed questioningly at her hands. She exclaimed, "It's wet! Everywhere I look, everything is wet. It looks like it's raining." Surely, this was evidence of the phrase below; *He will come to us like the rain:*

> *Let us know,*
> *Let us pursue the knowledge of the* LORD.
> *His going forth is established as the morning;*
> *He will come to us like the rain,*
> *Like the latter and former rain to the earth.*[11]

> *Sow for yourselves righteousness;*
> *Reap in mercy;*
> *Break up your fallow ground,*
> *For it is time to seek the* LORD,
> *Till He comes and rains righteousness on you.*[12]

My mother's experience is even more mind blowing in light of something the Lord had said to me a day or two earlier. I'd traveled to New Mexico where she was living with my sister, and had already been there longer than planned. Struggling to know whether to stay or to go home for a few days with my husband, the Lord woke me up around 3 AM one morning, and as I prayed I heard, "Trust me." I responded immediately, "Yes Lord, I will," and all question of leaving disappeared. Later, sitting beside her, out of the blue—or I should say, out of the heavens—I heard the Lord's voice speak gently, "This is my gift to you." Well, that sure sounded good, but what did it mean? Let me go back a bit for context.

When I first came to Aslan's Place and then became a prayer minister, the very idea caused my parents to think I'd gone off the deep end. As the years passed, there were a few opportunities to minister to family members, but I'd learned not to offend my parents' very solid traditional faith in God by sharing too much about my new encounters in the heavenly realms of the Spirit. Before Mom became so disabled that she could no longer be alone, I'd been her primary caregiver for five years after Dad's death as she lived independently, but from a wheelchair, a mile from my home in California. During that time, as happens for most of us who end up being parental caregivers, my role resembled more that of the parent and hers was of the child. This wasn't a situation that made me feel good, and when I was especially tired or frustrated I would often ask the Lord to please, please do something to transform my relationship with my mother; to please give me a way to remember her as my mom and not as a burdensome responsibility.

Fast-forward back to New Mexico. On my husband's birthday in August 2014, I'm the one who received the best gift, for that was the day that God answered my long-standing prayer about my mom. He made a way for me to lead my mother through several hours of deliverance; followed by an astonishing glory-filled time of worship that she led; followed by the manifestation of His rain. It's really a much longer story than fits here, because the miracles continued on throughout the final week of her life and her memorial services. One manifestation after another of His power occurred as the Lord multitasked, accomplishing miraculous things in my mother's life, while at the same time blessing my family and me beyond anything we could have imagined. Power manifested—definitely, His power!

13

CHAPTER THIRTEEN
The Rainbow Angel

Before we move too far away from the rain, let's consider rainbows. Following the awful finality of the flood that wiped everything from the face of the earth that was not inside of Noah's ark, God sent a rainbow, a manifestation of His power that is an eternal promise, or covenant:

> *And God said: "This is the sign of the covenant which I make between Me and you, and every living creature that is with you, for perpetual generations: I set My rainbow in the cloud, and it shall be for the sign of the covenant between Me and the earth. It shall be, when I bring a cloud over the earth, that the rainbow shall be seen in the cloud; and I will remember My covenant which is between Me and you and every living creature of all flesh; the waters shall never again become a flood to destroy all flesh. The rainbow shall be in the cloud, and I will look on it to remember the everlasting covenant between God and every living creature of all flesh that is on the earth." And God said to Noah, "This is the sign of the covenant which I have established between Me and all flesh that is on the earth."* [1]

It's a beautiful and extravagant promise, so no wonder the enemy has tried so hard to corrupt its image by using the rainbow as a symbol for homosexuality. But there's even more that I'm sure Satan doesn't want us to realize, for a rainbow angel is a spiritual servant of the Most High, and that undoubtedly causes much consternation within the enemy camp.

I saw still another mighty angel coming down from heaven, clothed with a cloud. And a rainbow was on his head, his face was like the sun, and his feet like pillars of fire.[2]

In the fall of 2013, while participating in a small home group Paul suddenly felt an arch on his head and wondered what it was. As they discussed what his new discernment could be, the realization came that it was the rainbow angel of Revelation 10:1.

In July 2014, and Paul was teaching in Moravian Falls. After reading from Daniel 7, he'd just finished reviewing the revelation about the clouds when he mentioned that he'd planned to stop there but that God was doing something new. Discerning the presence of a rainbow angel, he shared Revelation 10:1 and invited the participants to try to feel the angel. Then he continued on in the scripture to try to figure out what the Lord wanted them to understand:

He had a little book open in his hand. And he set his right foot on the sea and his left foot on the land, and cried with a loud voice, as when a lion roars. When he cried out, seven thunders uttered their voices. Now when the seven thunders uttered their voices, I was about to write; but I heard a voice from heaven saying to me, "Seal up the things which the seven thunders uttered, and do not write them."[3]

Paul commented, "I don't know what the little book in his hand is. I'm not happy yet, but the fact that we have revelation of the rainbow angel now would indicate that something has become unsealed. I think that's true. I think that's true."

The angel whom I saw standing on the sea and on the land raised up his hand to heaven and swore by Him who lives forever and ever, who created heaven and the things that are in it, the earth and the things that are in it, and the sea and the things that are in it, that there should be delay no longer.[4]

Paul said, "I want us to notice that last phrase; *There shall be delay no longer.* Isn't that what we've been hearing? I had a clue on Tuesday night when the speaker kept saying this is God's Kairos time. It's God's Kairos because it's not just time, but is the appointed time for what God wants to do. That's why my luggage arrived first—because there's going to be no more delay. Got that? The Lord liked it when I said that, I think. So keep on going:"

> *And the word of the LORD came to me, saying, "Son of man, what is this proverb that you people have about the land of Israel, which says, 'The days are prolonged, and every vision fails'"* [5]

"I believe this is a big deal. These are prophetic words that have not been fulfilled yet, and they are going to be fulfilled. That's what it says:"

> *Tell them therefore, 'Thus says the LORD GOD: "I will lay this proverb to rest, and they shall no more use it as a proverb in Israel."' But say to them, "The days are at hand, and the fulfillment of every vision. For no more shall there be any false vision or flattering divination within the house of Israel. For I am the LORD. I speak, and the word which I speak will come to pass; it will no more be postponed; for in your days, O rebellious house, I will say the word and perform it," says the LORD GOD.'"* [6]

"What was that? *It will no more be postponed.* There should be no more delay. Now go back to Revelation 10:7-11:"

> *But in the days of the sounding of the seventh angel, when he is about to sound, the mystery of God would be finished, as He declared to His servants the prophets. Then the voice which I heard from heaven spoke to me again and said, "Go, take the little book which is open in the hand of the angel who stands on the sea and on the earth." So I went to the angel and said to him, "Give me the little book." And he said to me, "Take and eat it; and it will make your stomach bitter, but it will be as sweet as honey in your mouth." Then I took the little book out of the angel's hand and ate it, and it was as sweet as honey in my mouth. But when I had eaten it, my stomach became bitter. And he said to me, "You must prophesy again about many peoples, nations, tongues, and kings."*

"So now we have the clouds, we have the rainbow angel who is coming wrapped in a cloud, and we have the breakthrough gate. [7] We went through the gate a few times before Rob Gross and I realized that the gate leads out, so you are breaking out into freedom with your king at your head. There are many peoples. Are you getting it? You are breaking out of Babylon, Egypt, bondage; you're breaking out of all the words that you've spoken against yourself and others have spoken against you."

In November 2014, Paul recorded his observations during a ministry session when the rainbow angel showed up with his little book. There was revelation that the book held math equations and geometric shapes that seemed to be equations of DNA and RNA, and when the angel showed up, the client's deliverance increased. Paul notes continue:

I am renewing your youth like an eagle. The original family lines are in this little book. The fallen sons of God came to earth early to mix up the family lines. The rainbow angel comes to adjust the family lines.

Clean off generations and times. Once it is cleaned, clean off the DNA. Ask the Lord to remove all evil off of the connection of the DNA to the human spirit.

The manifold wisdom of God is in our DNA…the enemy wanted to remove the manifold wisdom of God. There is some connection to the stars.

Do stars affect the DNA and RNA or program it?

I feel a fallen rainbow angel. He is slowing down time so that the end of days does not take place, and is controlling Greek time, which is circular. Time is trapped here so it does not flow where it is supposed to flow. This seems to be true for everyone. This would affect the prophetic fulfillment of persons.

It appears that the generational lines were formed in heaven and some of the family line came early and mated with the daughters of man, thus bringing parts of the generational lines into being too early, causing an eschewing of the line which resulted in a tension in the family line, which somehow affects time(s).

During a summit at Aslan's Place in February 2015, the Lord was moving us through heavenly places. Paul had been feeling healing, and he related what he was hearing in the realm to which we had come:

The rainbow angel's book; solution to man's problems; equations, geometric shapes, very, very complex; I am going to make the complex simple. Healing, wholeness, dignity, transformation is present in this realm.

As we continued in discernment and exploration, the conversation revolved around genetic contamination by the fallen sons of God and DNA coding. Then:

(Paul) The rainbow angel's book has all the codes.

I (Barbara) received a scroll and Paul told me to give it to Louise Hilby.[8]

(Paul) A rainbow angel is here.

(Louise, reading the scroll) This is by decree of the Holy Ones. I see the English, and then it flips to Hebrew. Something about not having gone this way before. The agreement with what you said about we begin, and we won't finish. I'm seeing the two strands have parted going into what I ate, going by the components, the base pairs, which would be the code. The code is going through the scrolls.

(Paul) I think this is part of the little book.

(Louise) It is for a time, not yet. He's giving us the knowledge because of the group. We are getting the new little bits. It is so.

And so we come back to God's perfect timing for the release of revelation and, even as this book is being written, our understand is increasing as He illuminates more of His truth.[9]

14

CHAPTER FOURTEEN

Confirming Visions

As we've seen, Paul first understood that clouds are spiritual beings in October 2013, and our prophetic words about the subject began in March 2009. At that time, Crystal Kain Ross was completely unaware of Aslan's Place. Though we are first cousins, we'd lost touch with one another for many years, re-connecting over the phone in 2010. Separated by well over 1500 miles, once Crystal understood that I wouldn't think she's crazy to hear clearly from the Lord, she began sending me hundreds of pages of documentation from her heavenly excursions. Her fantastic visions were astounding, so I began sharing bits and pieces with a few trusted friends, praying about them, and waiting to see if the Lord wanted me to pass them along to Paul. In March 2011, I began forwarding some messages for his consideration. Using an abundance of caution, Paul wisely consults others and carefully prays and ponders over everything he releases, so as we first began to talk about publishing Crystal's vision of the grid,[1] he shared it with Larry Pearson. Now, we know very well that Larry is a prophet, but it seems his response here was even more prophetic than any of us realized at the time. He emailed Paul:

> This is interesting to say the least. I'm left with the question, is this someone's mere prayer journal/assignment so God's purposes can be revealed on the earth? I don't feel anything negative. I just am not getting what to do about it all. Maybe someone else will have

understanding of the purpose of this. Could this just be a signpost on the road of revelation unfolding for something bigger down the road? As I typed that last bit, my spirit feels, "let it all simmer some more". These all are pieces to a larger puzzle. Perhaps premature release could give clues to the other camp what God is disclosing for a heavenly mandate?

A larger puzzle indeed! Once we started writing the *Exploring Heavenly Places* series, Crystal's visions and words began to find their places, illustrating time and again the ongoing revelation we are receiving. In this case, we review a vision from July 2009, the same year clouds began showing up around Aslan's Place, four years before Paul's ah-ha moment in New Jersey, and six years prior to the writing of this book. Her vision illustrates God's power as exhibited in the clouds, the lightnings, the unity and sense of wellbeing that occurs with the power manifestations of honey and oil, and she even answers my own question about what it would feel like to step out of a plane and walk on the clouds:

We were traveling very fast, but how fast? I don't know. It's hard to judge. Was it faster than the speed of light? Maybe, for as I looked around, I could see whole star systems whirring by with glorious colors and details that are beyond my ability to describe…Looming ahead, I saw a denser-than-normal, massive cloudbank full of glorious light, emerging toward me from the surrounding deep-space air. Was it moving toward me, or was I moving toward it? Somehow, it seemed as if both were moving toward each other…the massive cloud was round, but not perfectly round, being more oblong in the center than at the top and bottom. I could see into it, and as I came closer I noticed that the cloud was split into two parts, a top and bottom, and there were rays of lightning shooting like waves of liquid fire from it in a horizontal fashion from the opening…As I looked at the cloudbank, I knew there was something or someone very great and powerful in this cloud of light, and I knew that whatever was waiting for me inside was both a holy and hidden mystery…I was nearing the filtered-yet-tangible presence of the Most High God, whose name in Hebrew is El Elyon…The cloud itself seemed to be about the length of a football field and was perfectly cylindrical, with the angels spaced at all angles around its outside perimeter. Standing very near the outside, I observed that there were countless tiny arcing mini fires all surrounding both the outside and inside edges of the entire cloud. Though almost imperceptive, they were most beautiful, and a wonder in themselves. I could both see and hear them crackling with electrical currents like lightning bolts as they interacted with each other. They too, along with the angels, had a song they sung, and everything acted and reacted in total musical and spiritual harmony.

I did not know what the glory cloud floor would feel like. Would it feel solid, or would be more like walking on a semi-soft cloud blanket like the surface of the Power Grid feels to me. As it turned out, it was semi-solid, giving the feeling of walking on a cushion of nothing-yet-something, neither like a cloud nor a floor, but more like an air mattress that was floating in water without feeling squishy or sinking down…I walked further into the center of the expansive glory cloud on a surface that was perfect and a warm, my feet feeling wonderful as I walked deeper inside, finally stopping at about the middle. To describe what the surface felt like, I could only say that it was holy ground.

I looked at my hands and they were glowing with something that looked like glitter, but was wet like tiny drops of oil. I touched my hands and rubbed the glittering oil drops and they disappeared into my skin, making it feel as if I had just stood under a waterfall of God's pure love. I was entirely refreshed.

Over a seven-day period in June 2013, Crystal had a long series of heavenly experiences, excerpts of which are presented here because the close parallels to our ongoing exploration and revelation of the winds and the clouds. Keep in mind the fact that Crystal lives far away in a very remote area, and has no opportunity to participate in our various meetings. Her visions are not at all a result of anything we've learned but, as Larry surmised, appear to validate our findings after the fact.

The Lord had just introduced Crystal to the subject of matter, and her continuing visionary experience echoes our revelation regarding God's power. References are made to Him being our refuge from the storms, judgment, the winds, words as matter within a cloud, and lightnings:

Jesus said, "We have always used relatively small numbers of people to do great things, and this end-times task has never been done before, nor shall it be repeated again...As you are aware, the earth and all that surrounds it was created by Our spoken word.[2] You also know that everything We created was done using elements of matter as building blocks, and that words can be used as weapons. When released, they exhibit themselves in combinations of matter. The enemy also uses words, which are matter, to release his very limited and timed power against Our Light and those who love Us...It is time for you to be briefed as to the tasks at hand: Look, listen and learn...Observe!" Jesus boldly commanded, and with a sweep of His hand, He pulled back an invisible curtain. Now we were able to see air as both color and substance, and smell its various fragrances. Jesus continued, "What you are seeing is the actual wind. We have drawn back the normal barrier of your inability to see it, for the purpose of revealing to you what will shortly be done with Our secret and mysterious winds in the air. Write down these references as evidence." They are:

He causes the vapors to ascend from the ends of the earth;
He makes lightning for the rain;
He brings the wind out of His treasuries.[3]

You lift me up to the wind and cause me to ride on it;
You spoil my success.[4]

For He commands and raises the stormy wind,
Which lifts up the waves of the sea.[5]

Jesus picked up where He left off, "There are many types of winds and many elements that are propelled in air. Winds can be calming and pleasant. They cleanse and dust the earth. They bring refreshing. But they can also be destructive and bring great catastrophe... a very special wind will be released into the atmosphere. The supernatural winds, which have been prepared and kept in Our wind storehouses until this time, contain many matter elements, some very positive and some very negative combinations of matter. Once released, these mysterious, prophesied winds, will affect everyone who lives upon the earth. Know this! The release of these mysterious winds is a major part of the fulfillment of the mysteries of the seventh angel, which John saw and recorded in Revelation, but which have been sealed until now.[6] These promised winds shall bring one last final great awakening of light to the entire earth, and a great release of doom and judgment against the enemy. It will appear to many that darkness will win the final battle, and overcome all the saints. Many will lose their lives, and some who survive the transition will consider life to be futile and greatly wish to die. But this is exactly when the fulfillment shall come, for when those who have endured shall want to give up, Our supernatural winds will blow. Once the winds are released, it will be as if a super nova exploded, or a massive volcano erupted in the spiritual realm. The combinations of matter will be released into earth's atmosphere, and above earth's atmosphere into the heavens. Once there, they will continue to swirl the globe, and move as we have pre-determined, even reaching up into the outer areas of air surrounding the earth until time ceases to be…The winds will hold both judgment and mercy and many will come into the fold. Many will walk in very high realms of faith and function. It will become much more common-place for people to visit and accomplish their spiritual tasks on their own promised, and very real, high places.[7] For when you go through the waters, I will be with you, and when you endure great, fiery opposition, I will be your covering protection and refuge from the storms of lies.[8] At the same time, the elements of judgment matter against the enemy and darkness shall release overwhelming and destructive winds against their forces. Their might shall be greatly diminished; their effect shall wax and wane, but not stopped completely until time reaches its zero-point of existence."

I was sitting with Jesus standing on my right side. Then one of the angels walked over with an open Bible in his hand, and pointed down at a passage. He instructed me, "Don't forget to include these verses; they are very important."

He also established them forever and ever;
He made a decree which shall not pass away.
Fire and hail, snow and clouds;
Stormy wind, fulfilling His word.[9]

Then I heard the rumblings of great thunder from far away. As it echoed up into that vast ocean of blue-black space, the sounds were getting closer. It sounded like massive thunderous waves, mixed with canons, but was not like any thunder or sound waves I have heard before. It was beyond merely the sound of loud rumbling...I perceived a very distinctive and strong rumble, as well as enormous churning sounds. It was like the sound of great waters merging with the sounds of great wind...and looking towards the East, the direction the sound was coming from, observed the approach of a great, fiery, golden cloud enfolding upon itself in the far distance. It was so big. It seemed bigger than Jupiter...The main aspect of it other than billowing and enfolding was the great sizzling power resident within it, static electricity and bolts of lightning coursing throughout...

This cloud of power mesmerized me. I couldn't take my eyes off it...inside the cloud were so many colors that it was hard to count them all...Jesus said, "This cloud has been prepared to be the vehicle to carry the spiritual word 'atomic bomb', which shall usher in both favor and doom. This is not an ordinary cloud, for in fact it was prepared long ago. There will be other clouds and other elements of matter released, but there will never be another like this one. This is a pivotal event."

Then Jesus said, "Your spoken words will be the vehicle. As you speak them out loud, they will be placed inside"...I have to say it felt very odd to have Him tell us that when we spoke an element, it would physically be released into the cloud, but He said, "Do you not know that I move when words are spoken in faith? Faith words release My power...It really made me re-think praying for people by faith. To see the matter being released immediately with power and substance gave me even greater resolve to believe when I pray in the future.

And so it is clear; our direction comes as discernment and exploration, prophetic words and visions align with scriptural truth, and we move about in the heavenly realms by faith, according to the wisdom of Hebrews 11:1, 3:

Now faith is the assurance of things hoped for, the conviction of things not seen...By faith we understand that the universe was created by the word of God, so that what is seen was not made out of things that are visible.

15

CHAPTER FIFTEEN

Tardis

I woke up laughing. The Lord had shown me my Tardis. If you have not watched *Dr. Who*, the longest running television drama from the BBC in England, then you may not know about the Tardis. In order for Dr. Who to travel in space and time, he uses his Tardis as a spacecraft. From the outside it looks like an ordinary London telephone booth with typical dimensions, but the inside is huge and encompasses many floors. The main floor is a flight deck from which Dr. Who guides his spacecraft through time and space, and everyone who sees the Tardis comments, "It is bigger on the inside than the outside." Tardis is an acronym meaning, 'time and relative dimension in space'. When I woke up after seeing my Tardis I realized it was not a London telephone booth but an American one. As I looked, it was clear what the Lord was showing me. The Tardis was severely damaged, leaning on the front left side, having been through many wars in the dimensions. My dream took place in May 2014, only a few days after the Lord revealed a complicated territorial structure over the high desert during an Exploring Heavenly Places Exploration session, after which we asked the Lord to remove the evil system. Returning home, I learned that the side pain my wife, Donna, had experienced for several years had left, and it was totally gone until September of 2015. We are currently praying for the revelation that will result in a permanent healing.

A couple years after the first deliverance I led, the Lord gave me the idea of breaking all evil ties with the dimensions. I noticed that when I did this there was a marked change in the person and I could feel evil exiting their body, but I had no frame of reference for the prayer and was simply following the direction of the Spirit. During those years there was not much talk about the dimensions, but gradually sci-fi writers began incorporating the dimensional themes into their works. Scientists and mathematicians also formulated theories and mathematical equations that relied on the premise that there had to be dimensions to solve some of the mysteries of the universe. The concept of a multi-dimensional, multi-universe structure of the cosmos was taking shape. The idea of parallel universes[1] was also developing.

By this time, I had developed a strange dimensional experience in my body. While in Austin, Texas I'd started doing a pucker-sucking sound with the left side of my lips, and could not stop it throughout the ministry time. Returning home, Donna became concerned that I was developing a serious medical problem. While I assured her it was spiritual, I was not completely convinced. Some weeks later I began to understand that I was changing dimensions when my lips made that sound. Gradually, as I accepted the reality of this new discernment, the involuntary pull on the left side of my lips decreased to the point that I now notice only a slight pull on my lips and know that I am changing dimensions. As this is happening, I also now can hear a change notifying me that dimensions are shifting.

About five years ago, watching television in my home, I observed a sudden change in the atmosphere and what seemed to be the thick bottom of a Coca-Cola glass appeared in the right side of my vision. My sight was totally distorted on that side and I seriously wondered if I should go immediately to the emergency room. For over an hour, I observed as the distortion moved from right to left within my eye. After almost two hours, the blurriness disappeared and I felt normal again. This has now happened three times, and I have talked to others who have experienced the same phenomenon. My only explanation is that the Lord was moving us from one dimension to another.

In April 2015, I began wondering what the Bible actually said about the dimensions, the heavenly places, and thought I would develop a PowerPoint presentation of the biblical perspective of the dimensions. I was not prepared for what I was to discover. Searching the topic of 'heaven and heavens' in the Old Testament, I was stunned to see that every time those two words were written, 'heaven' in the original Hebrew was always plural. The translators often ignored this, rendering 'heavens' as 'heaven'. The Old Testament clearly describes a multi-dimensional creation. Looking at the New Testament, 'heavens' was often translated as heaven as well. Why had the translators ignored what the Greek actually conveyed?

Suddenly, I had a surprising grasp of revelation, and what I had not previously reconciled within our three-dimensional reality became crystal clear. The Biblical insight had been right in front of me, but I had not seen it. The dimensions, the heavenly places, contain secrets that open up our understanding of what many seers have spiritually perceived. There really are layers of reality in the heavenly places, and within those layers the great power of God exists.

16

CHAPTER SIXTEEN

The Heavens

I have been sharing abstract principles about the heavens, but the biblical text illustrates what the Lord has revealed. In fact, the first words of the Bible say that God created the heavens,[1] and several verses later scripture declares that there were lights in the expanse of the heavens. How many times had I read this verse without understanding what the Lord was saying? What was not clear has now become clear. God not only created lights in our three dimensional world, but He also created lights in the other heavenly places, the dimensions. These lights are not the same as those we see, but they are still lights—spiritual lights. I had discovered the first clue in a pattern that would be exposed throughout Old Testament; the reality that something in our three dimensional world is mirrored in a different way in many other dimensions. Let's explore other examples. Abraham is told:

> *"Look now toward heaven, and count the stars if you are able to number them." And He said to him, "So shall your descendants be."* [2]

The text actually should be translated "Look toward the heavens..." Not only are there physical stars, but it seems there are stars in other dimensions, lending understanding to Judges 5:20 where it was not the physical stars that fought, but it was spiritual stars from other heavenly places:

They fought from the heavens; the stars from their courses fought against Sisera.

There is fire in the dimensions, and perhaps different kinds of fire in different dimensions:[3]

Then you came near and stood at the foot of the mountain, and the mountain burned with fire to the midst of heaven(s), with darkness, cloud, and thick darkness.[4]

God speaks out of different dimensions:

Out of heaven(s) He let you hear His voice, that He might instruct you; on earth He showed you His great fire, and you heard His words out of the midst of the fire.[5]

There are different levels of the heavenly places, heaven's heavens:

Indeed heaven(s) and the highest heavens belong to the LORD your God, also the Earth with all that is in it.[6]

There are various kinds of rain that come from different dimensions, and both the Lord's curses and blessings originate in the heavens:

...lest the LORD's anger be aroused against you, and He shut up the heavens so that there be no rain, and the land yield no produce, and you perish quickly from the good land which the LORD is giving you.[7]

The LORD will open to you His good treasure, the heavens, to give the rain to your land in its season, and to bless all the work of your hand. You shall lend to many nations, but you shall not borrow.[8]

Warfare is not only in our reality, but exists in other heavenly places:

...the adversaries of the LORD shall be broken in pieces; from heaven(s) He will thunder against them. The LORD will judge the ends of the earth. He will give strength to His king, and exalt the horn of His anointed.[9]

There are not only physical birds but also birds in the spiritual realms:

The dogs shall eat whoever belongs to Jeroboam and dies in the city, and the birds of the air (heavens) shall eat whoever dies in the field; for the LORD has spoken! [10]

Our generational sin, or iniquities, is in the dimensions and is not confined to one spiritual realm. This explains the complexities of the deliverances that we experience:

At the evening sacrifice I arose from my fasting; and having torn my garment and my robe, I fell on my knees and spread out my hands to the LORD my God. And I said: "O my God, I am too ashamed and humiliated to lift up my face to You, my God; for our iniquities have risen higher than our heads, and our guilt has grown up to the heavens." [11]

There are vast spaces in the dimensions where we can be placed, and can be cast to the furthest places in the heavens. We can begin to understand how, in prayer ministry, we discover parts that are scattered in the length, width, height and depth:

...but if you return to Me, and keep My commandments and do them, though some of you were cast out to the farthest part of the heavens, yet I will gather them from there, and bring them to the place which I have chosen as a dwelling for My name. [12]

There are impurities in many of the dimensions:

If God puts no trust in His saints, And the heavens are not pure in His sight. [13]

There are laws in the heavens, not just in our visible heaven or in the spiritual heaven that we have believed God dwells in, but the heavens:

Do you know the ordinances of the heavens? Can you set their dominion over the earth? [14]

A multitude of waters exists in the heavens—many kinds of water in many kinds of dimensions:

When He utters His voice, There is a multitude of waters in the heavens: "And He causes the vapors to ascend from the ends of the earth. He makes lightning for the rain, He brings the wind out of His treasuries." [15]

Man can look not only into the physical heavens, but also into many dimensional places:

> *Now it came to pass in the thirtieth year, in the fourth month, on the fifth day of the month, as I was among the captives by the River Chebar, that the heavens were opened and I saw visions of God.*[16]

Before examining the word 'heaven' in the New Testament, I had assumed that I would not see the same pattern as the Old Testament because we have been conditioned to think of heaven in the singular tense. The one exception of which I was aware is when the Apostle Paul explains that we are seated with Christ in the heavenly places.[17] My belief was challenged when I looked at the original Greek and found there were many places where the correct translation would be 'heavens' rather than 'heaven'.

When John the Baptist saw Jesus he declared the kingdom of the heavens was at hand, not the kingdom of heaven:

> *In those days John the Baptist came preaching in the wilderness of Judea, and saying, "Repent, for the kingdom of heaven(s) is at hand!" For this is he who was spoken of by the prophet Isaiah, saying: "The voice of one crying in the wilderness: 'Prepare the way of the LORD; Make His paths straight.'"*[18]

The poor in spirit do not inherit the kingdom of heaven but the kingdom of the heavens:

> *Blessed are the poor in spirit, For theirs is the kingdom of heaven(s).*[19]

Our reward is in the heavenly places, not in heaven:

> *Rejoice and be exceedingly glad, for great is your reward in heaven(s), for so they persecuted the prophets who were before you.*[20]

When Jesus spoke of the kingdom of heaven He was really speaking about the kingdom of the heavens. The emphasis is on the heavens, and not the heaven:

> *Whoever therefore breaks one of the least of these commandments, and teaches men so, shall be called least in the kingdom of heaven(s); but whoever does and teaches them, he shall be called great in the kingdom of heaven(s). For I say to you, that unless your righteousness exceeds the righteousness of the scribes and*

Pharisees, you will by no means enter the kingdom of heaven.[21]

Take heed that you do not do your charitable deeds before men, to be seen by them. Otherwise you have no reward from your Father in heaven(s). Therefore, when you do a charitable deed, do not sound a trumpet before you as the hypocrites do in the synagogues and in the streets, that they may have glory from men. Assuredly, I say to you, they have their reward.[22]

The Lord's Prayer speaks of both heaven and the heavens, and the last use of heaven is singular:

In this manner, therefore, pray: Our Father in heaven(s), hallowed be Your name. Your kingdom come. Your will be done on earth as it is in heaven.[23]

We are to proclaim that the heavens are here:

And as you go, preach, saying, "The kingdom of heaven(s) is at hand." Heal the sick, cleanse the lepers, raise the dead, cast out demons. Freely you have received, freely give.[24]

When we are humble we are great in the heavens:

Therefore whoever humbles himself as this little child is the greatest in the kingdom of heaven(s).[25]

The Son of Man came down from heaven (singular) but He is in the heavens (plural).

No one has ascended to heaven but He who came down from heaven, that is, the Son of Man who is in heaven.[26]

Jesus is the only name under the heavens:

Nor is there salvation in any other, for there is no other name under heaven(s) given among men by which we must be saved.[27]

Jesus, our Master, is in the heavens:

And you, masters, do the same things to them, giving up threatening, knowing that your own Master also is in heaven(s), and there is no partiality with Him.[28]

Our citizenship is in the heavens:

> *For our citizenship is in heaven(s), from which we also eagerly wait for the Savior, the Lord Jesus Christ.*[29]

Our hope is laid up in the heavens:

> *...because of the hope which is laid up for you in heaven(s), of which you heard before in the word of the truth of the gospel.*[30]

We wait for Jesus to come from the heavens:

> *...and to wait for His Son from heaven(s), whom He raised from the dead, even Jesus who delivers us from the wrath to come.*[31]

Our inheritance is stored up in the heavens:

> *to an inheritance incorruptible and undefiled and that does not fade away, reserved in heaven(s) for you, who are kept by the power of God through faith for salvation ready to be revealed in the last time.*[32]

I had made my way all the way to the last book of the New Testament, Revelation, where I counted 49 times that heaven was used in the singular and only once in the plural.[33] Fifty reminds me of the number for year of jubilee, so a question still fills my mind. Why is the word used singularly so many times in the book of Revelation?

Though this volume is about power in the heavenly places, there is apparently much more we need to learn about these dimensions and how to access God's power from all of them. And so, our journey continues.

ENDNOTES

Chapter 1: *Discerning God's Power*

1   Acts 4:32–35

Chapter 2: *The Manifestat Power of God*

1   http://dictionary.reference.com/browse/power
2   Philippians 3:10-11

Chapter 3: *A Taste of Honey*

1   Psalm 119:103
2   Exodus 16:31
3   Isaiah 13:2-8
4   Ezekiel 3:3, Revelation 10:9-10
5   Proverbs 16:24
6   Mimi Lowe is a prayer minister, an author, and a member of the board of Joel's Well Ministries. Her website is http://www.mimilowe.com
7   Beelzebub in Hebrew is literally, 'Lord of the Flies' per http://en.wikipedia.org/wiki/Beelzebub
8   1 Samuel 14:25-28
9   Proverbs 24:13-14, 25:16, 25:27
10   Song of Solomon 4:11, 5:1, Proverbs 5:3
11   Crystal Kain Ross is Barbara's cousin and is a prophetic intercessor and friend of Aslan's Place.
12   Deuteronomy 32:13
13   Exodus 3:8, 3:17, 13:5, 33:3, Leviticus 20:24, Numbers 13:27, 14:8, 16:13, 16:14, Deuteronomy 6:3, 11:9, 26:9,26:15, 27:3, 31:20, Joshua 5:6, Jeremiah 11:5, 32:22, Ezekiel 20:6, 20:15
14   Genesis 43:11, Deuteronomy 8:7-9, 2 Kings 18:32, Ezekiel 16:3, Ezekiel 27:17
15   Isaiah 7:14-24
16   Matthew 16:24

Chapter 4: *God's Weather Report*

1   Luke 12:54-56
2   Ecclesiastes 1:4-7

3 Job 36: 26-33

4 Ezekiel 13:13

5 Psalm 107:25-29

6 Mark 4:39, 41

7 Revelation 7:1

8 Larry Pearson is co-founder of Lion's Sword Communications. He is a co-founder and board member of Joel's Well Ministries. His website is http://lionsword.ca

9 Dawn Bray is a prayer minister and prophetic intercessor. Her website is http://newreflection ministries.org

10 Exodus 20:18-20

11 Isaiah 41:10

Chapter 5: *The Power of Whirlwinds*

---

1 http://www.invubu.com/lyrics/show/Kevin_Prosch/Show_Your_Power.html

2 The revelation of the golden pipes will be discussed in detail in *Exploring Heavenly Places, Volume 5*

3 Ezekiel 1:4

4 Patterson, R. D. (1999). 1478 סוּפ. (R. L. Harris, G. L. Archer Jr., & B. K. Waltke, Eds.) *Theological Wordbook of the Old Testament*. Chicago: Moody Press.

5 Patterson, R. D. (1999). 1528 רַעַס. (R. L. Harris, G. L. Archer Jr., & B. K. Waltke, Eds.) *Theological Wordbook of the Old Testament*. Chicago: Moody Press.

6 Other key scriptures on the whirlwind: Jeremiah 4:13, Jeremiah 23:18-20, Jeremiah 25:31-38, Jeremiah 30:23, Ezekiel 1:4-5, Hosea 8:7, Nahum 1:2-15, Psalm 97

7 Job 37:9–13

8 Proverbs 1:27-33

9 Proverbs 10:25

10 Isaiah 17:13

11 Isaiah 40:24

12 Isaiah 66:14-16

Chapter 6: *Unfolding Revelation of Whirlwinds*

---

1 Robin Shannon is a prayer minister, a prophetic dancer, and teaches classes on worship expression

2 Jana Green is an artist, a prayer minister, and a prophetic intercessor. Her website is http://www.signsandwondersstudio.com

3 Persis Tiner is a prayer minister and prophetic intercessor. She is a board member of Joel's Well Ministries.

4 Rob Gross is the pastor of Mountain View Community Church in Kaneohe, Hawaii, and is co-author of *Exploring Heavenly Places, Volume II, Revealing the sons of God.*

Chapter 7: *The Lightnings of God*

1   Psalm 18:14

2   Psalm 144:5-6

3   The Baptism of the Holy Ghost Part 1. John G. Lake. February 23, 1921 Edited/ Abridged by Tentmaker Ministries.

Chapter 8: *Unfolding Revelation of Lightnings*

1   Come Up Higher by Paul Cox...

2   Ann Bower is a prophetic intercessor, prayer minister and longtime friend of Aslan's Place

3   Romans 8:11

4   Job 37:2-4

5   Lewis

6   Raylene Zendejas is a prophetic intercessor and longtime friend of Aslan's Place

7   2 Samuel 22:14-16

8   Psalm 77:18

9   Psalm 97:3-4

10 Nahum 3:4

11 Zechariah 9:14

12 Jeremiah 10:13 and 51:16

13 Ezekiel 1:4-6, 9, 12-14

Chapter 9: *Introduction to Clouds*

1   1 Kings 18:45

2   Job 26:8-9

3   Job 35:5

4   Job 37:14-16

5   Psalm 77:17

6   Psalm 147:8

7   Exodus 13:21

8   2 Samuel 22:10-*13*

9   Job 22:14

10 Psalm 97:2

11 Psalm 18:11

12 Psalm 104:3

13 Ezekiel 30:3

14 Joel 2:1b-2a

15 Zephaniah 1:15
16 Ezekiel 1:28
17 Matthew 24:30
18 Hebrews 12:1-2
19 Revelation 14:14-16

Chapter 10: *Unfolding Revelation of Clouds*

1   Paul Knight is a composer in the theater district of London, England. With his wife, Jan, he oversees Aslan's Place, London, and is also a member of the board of directors of Joel's Well Ministries.

Chapter 11: *The Cloud of Witnesses*

1   Hebrews 12:1-2
2   Revelation 8:1
3   Hebrews 12:18-24

Chapter 12: *The Rain*

1   Genesis 2:4-6
2   Genesis 7:4
3   Genesis 7:12
4   Deuteronomy 11:16-17
5   Leviticus 26:3-4
6   Deuteronomy 28:12
7   Deuteronomy 32:1-3
8   Isaiah 45:8
9   1 Samuel 12:17-18
10   Psalm 68:7-9,14
11   Hosea 6:3
12   Hosea 10:12

Chapter 13: *The Rainbow Angel*

1   Genesis 9:12-17
2   Revelation 10:1
3   Revelation 10:2-4
4   Revelation 10:5-6
5   Ezekiel 12:21-22
6   Ezekiel 12:23-25

7   Breakthrough will be discussed in detail in *Exploring Heavenly Places, Volume 5.*

8   Louise Hilby is a prophetic intercessor and a long-time friend of Aslan's Place.

9   When completed, *Exploring Heavenly Places, Volume 5* will include more revelatory messages from rainbow angels.

Chapter 14: *Confirming Visions*

1   Crystal's vision of the grid is in *Exploring Heavenly Places, Volume 3*

2   Genesis 1:3

3   Psalm 135:7

4   Job 30:22

5   Psalm 107:25

6   Revelation 10:7

7   Habakkuk 3:19

8   Isaiah 43:2, Daniel 3:25, Psalms 91

9   Psalm 148:6,8

Chapter 15: *Tardis*

1   The structure of the multiverse, the nature of each universe within it and the relationships among the various constituent universes, depend on the specific multiverse hypothesis considered. Multiple universes have been hypothesized in cosmology, physics, astronomy, religion, philosophy, transpersonal psychology, and fiction, particularly in science fiction and fantasy. In these contexts, parallel universes are also called "alternate universes", "quantum universes", "interpenetrating dimensions", "parallel dimensions", "parallel worlds", "alternate realities", "alternate timelines", and "dimensional planes", among other names. The American philosopher and psychologist William James coined the term *multiverse* in 1895, but in a different context.   http://www.wikipedia.org/wiki/Multiverse

Chapter 16: *The Heavens*

1   Genesis 1:1, *In the beginning God created the heavens and the earth.* Psalm 96:5; Colossians 1:16; Hebrews 1:10; 2 Peter 3:5

2   Genesis 15:5

3   *(s)* has been added to the appropriate succeeding verses to indicate the proper plural translation

4   Deuteronomy 4:11

5   Deuteronomy 4:36

6   Deuteronomy 10:14, and see also 2 Chronicles 2:6 and Nehemiah9: 6

7   Deuteronomy 11:17, and see also 1 Kings 8:35, 2 Chronicles 6:26, 2 Chronicles 7:13,

Psalm 8:8, Psalm 68:8

8   Deuteronomy 28:12

9   1 Samuel 2:10

10   1 Kings 14:11–12

11   Ezra 9:5–6

12   Nehemiah 1:9

13   Job 15:15

14   Job 38:33

15   Jeremiah 10:13, and see also Jeremiah 51:16

16   Ezekiel 1:1

17   Ephesians 2:6

18   Matthew 3:1–3

19   Matthew 5:3

20   Matthew 5:12

21   Matthew 6:1–2

22   Matthew 5:19–20, and see also Matthew 22:1–3, Matthew 23:13

23   Matthew 6:9–10

24   Matthew 10:7–8

25   Matthew 18:4

26   John 3:13

27   Acts 4:12

28   Ephesians 6:9

29   Philippians 3:20

30   Colossians 1:5

31   1 Thessalonians 1:10

32   1 Peter 1:4–5

33   Revelation 12:12, *Therefore rejoice, O heavens, and you who dwell in them! Woe to the inhabitants of the earth and the sea! For the devil has come down to you, having great wrath, because he knows that he has a short time.*